"The importance of the letter of James to the church in Africa is not lost on anyone who is interested in the development of Christianity on the continent. This is a letter that speaks to contemporary African socio-economic and political realities. Readers will find in Adewuya's simple but profound volume studies on what a portion of the Scriptures has to teach us about the relationship between faith and the public sphere in contemporary Africa."

—KWABENA ASAMOAH-GYADU, Trinity Theological Seminary

"Drawing on the resources of African proverbs and stories, as well as his personal experience, Adewuya spotlights the pastoral and formational message of the letter of James. But this commentary is not just for Africans. Adewuya's sensitivity to the letter's communal dimension and to its message of hope for the marginalized will enable Western Christian to read James more faithfully. If you are looking for an outstanding example of contextual interpretation that remains faithful to the biblical text, this book is for you!"

—DEAN FLEMMING, MidAmerica Nazarene University, emeritus

"Adewuya has filled in a hole on our bookshelves that many of us may never have known we had. In a commentary that is exegetical and scholarly, he models exegeting well through story, through history, and through the experience of the African peoples. This is a commentary for the community."

—MARIAM KOVALISHYN, Regent College

"This book is much more than an interpretation of the letter of James for African contexts. Adewuya's use of African language translations and his applications of this letter's lessons for Africa illumine the text for all readers. These interpretive moves provide a clearer understanding of its meaning for its original readers and bring its message alive for present-day readers. Adewuya has given readers of James a great gift."

—JERRY L. SUMNEY, Lexington Theological Seminary

"In this volume, Adewuya draws on his multi-decadal life in Africa, his vast international pastoral experience, and his impeccable academic New Testament training to produce an African commentary on the letter of James. Offering a careful reading of the text, Adewuya draws heavily on the African reception (history) of James with much profit. By this means, the author pushes the global conversation about the New Testament forward in helpful and concrete ways."

—JOHN CHRISTOPHER THOMAS, Pentecostal Theological Seminary

"Adewuya invites us to listen with him to the letter of James as it speaks to an African context. Readers will particularly appreciate his attention to cultural intertexture, as he sets the wisdom of James alongside and in conversation with the pithy maxims encapsulating facets of the wisdom of several African peoples, seating James at a place of honor within the local council of elders."

—DAVID A. DESILVA, Ashland Theological Seminary

An African Commentary
on the Letter of James

GLOBAL READINGS

Interpreters of scripture have come increasingly to recognize the importance of engaging interpretations of the biblical texts from contexts other than their own. Reading merely from within our own social location risks being inadequate to perceive the formational promise and challenge of scriptural texts fully, for the lenses placed over our eyes by our social location, its ideologies, and its interests cloud our perception of many points at which the biblical texts might most challenge what we have come to accept as the "givenness" of those ideologies and interests. Listening to readings from multiple social locations allows us to triangulate beyond the blinders of our own social location, to perceive more the vision for discipleship and life together in the text, to hear more fully its challenge to us within our social location.

Volumes in *Global Readings* are written from the conviction that solid historical exegesis is, first and foremost, an exercise in cross-cultural hermeneutics applied to a text written in a foreign language from a foreign location with a political system, ideologies, economics, social institutions, and religious cultures profoundly different from our own. Rejecting the easy identification of historical exegesis as "Eurocentric," it is engaged rather as a means by which to listen patiently to the text within its own context and beyond the interference of the assumptions and impositions of our own context as much as possible. The fruits of this study are then put into dialogue with the social, economic, political, and ideological realities of the interpreter and his or her community, listening to how the concerns, questions, and wisdom of the foreign text interacts with and addresses the interpreter's context. Each volume, in turn, is offered to the broader interpretive community as a means by which to perceive new questions that we did not know the text was asking of us and new challenges that we did not realize the text was posing. In this manner, both traditional exegesis and social location hermeneutics contribute to uncovering how a text can challenge the assumptions and diagnose the blind spots that obscure the formational potential of the biblical text in any social location.

David A. deSilva, *series editor*

An African Commentary on the Letter of James

Global Readings

J. AYODEJI ADEWUYA

CASCADE *Books* • Eugene, Oregon

AN AFRICAN COMMENTARY ON THE LETTER OF JAMES

Global Readings

Cascade Books
An Imprint of Wipf and Stock Publishers
199 W. 8th Ave., Suite 3
Eugene, OR 97401

www.wipfandstock.com

PAPERBACK ISBN: 978-1-4982-8438-7
HARDCOVER ISBN: 978-1-4982-8440-0
EBOOK ISBN: 978-1-4982-8439-4

Cataloguing-in-Publication data:

Names: Adewuya, J. Ayodeji, author.

Title: An African commentary on the Letter of James / J. Ayodeji Adewuya.

Description: Eugene, OR: Cascade Books, 2023 | Global Readings | Includes bibliographical references.

Identifiers: ISBN 978-1-4982-8438-7 (paperback) | ISBN 978-1-4982-8440-0 (hardcover) | ISBN 978-1-4982-8439-4 (ebook)

Subjects: LCSH: Bible. James—Commentaries—Africa. | Bible. James—Criticism, interpretation, etc.—Africa.

Classification: BS2785.53 A349 2023 (paperback) | BS2785.53 (ebook)

01/17/23

To my precious grandchildren,
Deborah Grace Olufunmilayo and *Theodore James Ayobami*,
born in the diaspora

CONTENTS

PREFACE

My INTEREST IN THE letter of James stems from its perceived second-fiddle role to the letters of Paul, even in course offerings in most seminaries. It was an interest that led me to start teaching a course on James every two years. Selecting textbooks for the course further opened my eyes to the need for this present work which, hopefully, can serve as a supplementary textbook to other scholarly works on James. Although there are few journal articles and essays written by non-Western scholars, one could count such works from the majority world on one's fingers. Scholarly commentaries on the same are almost nonexistent. Providentially, Dr. David deSilva graciously invited me to write a commentary on James as part of the Global Readings on the New Testament, bringing to bear my African heritage. It has been a great pleasure working with him during the editorial process.

The writing of this commentary is a validation of the Yoruba proverb, *agbajowo la fi n soya, ajinjin owo kan ko gbe'ru d'ori* (one hand cannot adequately lift a load to the head). It speaks of the importance of collaboration. To make the book as "African" as possible, I established a James study group in Nigeria, giving an opportunity to "ordinary readers," that is, non-scholars, to read the letter and share what they heard as they read. The input of the study group on James has made the book richer. I also consulted with other Christians from other parts of Africa to test my ideas.

My special thanks go to the board of trustees of the Pentecostal Theological Seminary for granting me a sabbatical leave to complete the writing of this project for which I spent a previous one doing research. Thanks to Asbury Theological Seminary for providing me with free lodging during one week of research. I am also grateful to the Nazarene Theological

College, Manchester, for granting me the privilege to present the book's first chapter as the guest speaker at their theology conference in 2019. This is in addition to providing me with free accommodation for research on this and other projects in January 2019. I am very grateful to all who contributed in different ways to the completion of the book.

INTRODUCTION

An African Contextual Reading of the Letter of James

WRITING A COMMENTARY ON James was the last thing on my mind. That is not an uncharacteristic statement about a book that has functioned as a "sidekick" to Paul's letters for centuries. However, the invitation forced me to reflect both on the neglect of the book of James and that of Africa. James resonates with the African situation on various levels. First is its history of reception. James's history of reception is parallel to the story of the peoples on the African continent. Africa has been a sidekick in global affairs—socio-economic, political, theological education and scholarship, and other matters. It is a continent used to further various agendas apart from its own. Africa is called upon only when necessary, in the circumstances ranging from being used as military bases to the testing of new pharmaceutical drugs or as dumping ground for Western goods.

James, like Africa, is still trying to find its voice from an African context.[1] James has often been "exploited" for its relevance to Christian ethics and its importance for understanding the relationship between faith and works. Until recent years in New Testament scholarship, James has been voiceless, yearning to be understood on its own apart from its theological relationship to the Gospels and the letters of Paul. In that context, this commentary wants to articulate the message of James, using the voice of an

---

1. As Mariam Kamell notes in her excellent review of Gowler's commentary on James, the voices of Africans and Asians remain strangely silent, "even while liberation and feminist voices are highlighted and given priority." See "Review of James through the Centuries," 546.

1

African. I aim to pursue this task fully convinced that the Scriptures are read and interpreted within specific cultural contexts. It is a contextual reading.

A few explanations are in order to posit a contextual reading of James as an African. First, my primary focus will be on what an ordinary African reader hears when reading the text. Rather than focusing on the world "behind the text" for the historical situations that gave rise to it and the resources that went into it, or reading to discover the world "within the text," that is, a literary approach. This book is chiefly interested in the readers' appropriation of the text. The task here is to read James in its original context and show how some Africans do so from their context. It attempts an inclusive reading that discovers the voice of the marginalized in the text and their context. Most of the African examples in this book are from my reflection, personal experience, and interactions with other Africans. As part of writing this commentary, I formed a study group in Nigeria to read the book of James and provide feedback, some of which is incorporated into this commentary. I also had the privilege of discussing James with students and pastors from East Africa, particularly from Kenya, during several visits to Nairobi. The fundamental question posed to them was to know what they "heard" when James was read, to know how James spoke to them in their social location. Hence, the approach of this commentary is not to provide a detailed verse-by-verse historico-grammatical analysis of James, a task that many scholars have done excellently well. My task is to proffer my reflections on the book of James as an African.

Second, James resonates with the African situation on the sociocultural level. Important in this regard is the communal dimension of James, which, until recently, has been ignored and insufficiently explored. Often, James is read as a letter about the practice of each person rather than about the formation of a kind of community. This, of course, is largely due to the Reformation and Protestant emphasis on individual salvation. However, whatever attention James focuses on the individuals or even subgroups within the community, it is the community that provides the context for his moral and ethical appeals. As Hartin rightly notes, "the individual is addressed only where he or she is part of the community."[2] The community is the matrix within which individual lives of faith are nurtured and maintained. James strives diligently to maintain and build up the communal fellowship. The role of the community in African ethics is well summed up by John Taylor. He writes:

> Every man is born into a community. He is a member of a family
> and grows up inheriting certain family characteristics, certain
> property, certain obligations; he learns certain family traditions,

2. Hartin, *James*, 4.

certain patterns of behavior, and certain points of pride. In the same way, also, he is a member of a particular clan, tribe and nation, and these will give him a particular culture and history, and a particular way of looking at things, probably a particular religion. It is in such ways that every human being belongs to his environment. . . . Men and women who do not live in a community and feel that they really belong to it are not completely human. Something essential is missing, something which God has ordained for them as necessary for their authentic life. "It is not good for the man to be alone" (Gen 2:18).[3]

Third, in terms of its literary form, a distinct feature of James is its noted affinity with wisdom literature. The book contains sayings, aphorisms, and proverbs that are like the use of proverbs and stories in African tradition. Although Turner's assessment of the literary form of James is open to question, he is undoubtedly correct that "the pithy disconnected form and the frequency of aphorisms, epigrams and similes, appeals to the proverbs-loving African Christian, and the practical nature of the contents is completely in line with his own conception of religion."[4] Proverbs are sprinkled into conversations in Africa. Pithy statements are used to teach values and make astute observations about everything from human nature to wise living to the role of women in society. An aptly spoken proverb is met with approval in the courts of kings and the courtyards of mothers admonishing their children. In keeping with this, the reader will notice the use of African proverbs, sayings, and examples throughout this commentary to shed light on the text's reception in an African context.

Fourth, on the religious level, James, arguably more than any other book in the New Testament canon, best encapsulates the issues facing peoples of Africa and the churches in particular. Going by the standards of the Western world, the average Christian in Africa—like the average person in Africa—is poor. Hence, the book is much at home and often cited in contexts of spiritual healing, persecution, oppression, resistance, activism and social justice, and even interfaith relations. The dominant and pervasive presence of poverty promotes awareness of the transience of life, the dependence of individuals and nations on God, and distrust of the secular order.

Fifth, on the politico-economic level, the book of James is much at home among African readers because such familiar pressing problems mark the world it describes as famine and plague, oppression, persecution, poverty and exile, patronage, clientelism, and corruption. A poor readership

---

3. Taylor, *Christianity and Politics in Africa*, 35.
4. Turner, *Profile through Preaching*, 49.

can readily identify with James's audience of peasants and small crafts-people dominated by powerful landlords and imperial forces, by debit and credit networks. Philip Jenkins is right on target that in African societies, "the excruciating poverty of 'Lazarus eating the crumbs beneath the rich man's table' is not just an archaeological curiosity."[5] It is indeed real, and the more possible it is to identify the African situation with the *Sitz-im-Leben* of James, the clearer it becomes that the book is not just a historical artifact but one that is relevant to daily conduct. On its cover of May 11, 2000, *The Economist* featured "Hopeless Africa." The continent's problems are legion and widespread. African countries fill twenty-eight of the bottom thirty places of the UN's 2015 Human Development Index, based on a range of quality-of-life indicators.[6] James provides immediate and often material an-swers to life's problems. It teaches ways to cope and survive in a hostile en-vironment and at the same time holds out the hope of victory in the future. For the growing churches of the South, the Bible speaks to everyday issues of poverty and debt, famine and urban crisis, racial and gender oppression, state brutality, and persecution.

AUTHORSHIP

Although the letter itself identifies the name of its author as James (1:1), the specific identification of James remains unresolved because of several individuals named James in the New Testament. Two of those belonged to the Twelve (Mark 3:16–19), James the son of Zebedee and James the son of Alphaeus, and the others included "James the younger" or "James "the little one" (Mark 15:40), James the Father of Judas Thaddaeus (Luke 6:16), and James the brother of Judas (that is, Jude), who is also the brother of Jesus, possibly the very one designated in the superscription in chapter 1, verse 1 of the Epistle of James as, "James, a servant of God and of the Lord Jesus Christ."

John Calvin argued for James, the brother of John, who was executed during the reign of Herod Agrippa around AD 44, thus predating the likely timeframe of the letter's composition. There is no evidence for this

5. Jenkins, *New Faces of Christianity*, 68.

6. For one to talk about "Africa" as opposed the diverse countries which make up the continent in the context of the current situation can be misleading. That's partly because good news about Africa rarely makes headlines, even though the continent has its share of success stories. Sierra Leone, Liberia, Côte d'Ivoire, Mozambique, and Rwanda have disappeared from the international headlines for all the right reasons, with impressive transformations to peace and relative stability. Ghana, Senegal, Na-mibia, and Botswana, among others, have also quietly acquired a reputation for good governance and for building stable democracies.

authorship elsewhere, particularly in Acts.[7] Following some principles of elimination based on the history of tradition, as McKnight suggests, there are only three different feasible candidates for authorship: James, the brother of Jesus, another individual under the pseudonym of the brother of Jesus, or yet an anonymous individual[8] who might or might not have had any connections to James the apostle.

Paul recognizes James's role and importance in the Jerusalem church (Gal 1:15–2:12). Paul's mission caused concerns outside Jerusalem where his work was successful, which explains the emissaries from James who came to Antioch and successfully exerted pressure on Peter and Barnabas (Gal 2:12–13). Douglas J. Moo presents the case for James, "the brother of the Lord," who was not a prominent follower of Jesus until after the resurrection, as documented in 1 Cor 15:7 and John 7:5. He consequently played a leading role in the early church setting. Moo argues that "none of the other Jameses mentioned in the New Testament lived long enough or was prominent enough to write the letter we have before us without identifying himself any further than he does."[9] This is the position adopted in this commentary.

DATE

If James, the brother of Jesus, wrote this letter, it must have been written before his martyrdom in AD 62.[10] Another factor to be considered is the socio-economic restraints of that period. Peter H. Davids rightly points out that the very socio-economic structure of the society and the church itself was indicative of the severe economic need in Jerusalem in the forties. James addressed such issues and struggles in the early church that was at least fifteen years old and was already struggling with 'worldliness.' Thus, the decade of the forties is likely to be the timeframe when some of the contents of the letter were in oral circulation before it was recorded in its entire final form, possibly at a later stage.[11]

7. Osborne, "James, 1–2 Peter, Jude," 3.

8. McKnight, Letter of James, 13–15.

9. Moo, Letter of James, 9–10.

10. Josephus Flavius, the Jewish historian, in Antiquities 20.9.1 refers to the death of James, brother of Jesus. He states, " . . . Festus was now dead, and Albinus was but upon the road; so he assembled the sanhedrim of judges, and brought before them the brother of Jesus, who was called Christ, whose name was James, and some others; and when he had formed an accusation against them as breakers of the law, he delivered them to be stoned . . ."

11. David, Commentary on James, 9.

There is still a need to determine the date of the composition of the document as a final product. In chapter 2, James addresses justification, thus showing familiarity with Paul's teaching of "justification by faith." Another indication that speaks in favor of the relatively early composition is James's apparent unawareness of the conflict over the teaching of Torah on circumcision as related to the gentile mission, which was most probably the prevailing concern around and after the apostolic council. Based on these arguments, Moo proposes the middle forties as the date of the letter's composition, thus preceding both the council and the turbulent times of the Jewish rebellion in AD 66–70.[12] McKnight opts for a more flexible time-frame, "anytime from the middle 40s of the first century into the middle of the second century, proper nuances aside" (most reasonably in the fifties, the evidence being favorable and not ultimately conclusive), pointing out that the argument of Torah observance links the author to possibly both early and later Jewish Christian tradition. The lack of references to Christology does not imply early dating.[13]

RECIPIENTS

To sketch James's addressees, one must consider the social-political-religious makeup of the early Christians in the first century AD. Assuming that the letter was written in the fifties, Witherington analyzes the audience's social fabric, stating that the original recipients were members of the Jewish Christian community in Jerusalem, and possibly to "a few Jewish Christians whom Paul had managed to convert through his preaching in the diaspora synagogues (2 Cor 11:24)" who were, mostly, marginalized. A couple of Jewish Christians (Peter being one of them) had already been jailed by this time, while James, the son of Zebedee, died a martyr's death. Famine and food shortages were not unusual occurrences. Hence, James's appeals not to neglect the poor and a tendency towards communitarianism. Amidst persecution, famine, poverty, and the rising social tensions and religious pressure, James deals with wealth and poverty.[14]

Pedrito U. Maynard-Reid draws attention to the danger of reading our modern conceptions of class system into the social milieu of the time. In this sense, one ought not simply to suppose the existence of a strong middle class in urban settings. Indeed, the Hellenistic period brought forth some advancement in agriculture, industry, commerce, etc. (features which

12. Moo, *Letter of James*, 25–27.

13. McKnight, *Letter of James*, 35, 36–38.

14. Witherington, *Letters and Homilies for Jewish Christians*, 401–5.

intertwined with those of the period of the early Roman Empire). Yet only a few benefited from economic growth, with the gap between the upper and lower classes becoming increasingly noticeable. Maynard-Reid concludes, "thus it becomes more and more clear that it was not merely political dissatisfaction or religious fanaticism that brought unrest throughout the empire. The root cause of the misery was economic."[15] It was a period of socio-economic and religious turmoil, with a very pronounced gap between the elite and the poor, thus creating an unbalanced and disproportionately tailored socio-economic stratification.[16] Theissen expands on this by observing that ". . . the fronts between different classes were never entirely clear-cut. There were rival parties in the upper classes themselves."[17]

The overall challenge was even more daunting for the Christianized Jews, struggling to find the *via media,* as distinct from both Judaism and the Roman/Hellenistic cultural matrix. James was attempting to provide some identity guidelines (particularly ethical and moral) for the clear (re)definition of the Christian Jewish congregations over against non-Christian Jews and Hellenized Jews as a whole, for only such a (re)definition would prevent them from assimilating in the environment that was rather hostile in many regards.[18] Perdue underlines the comforting character of the letter: amid present suffering, struggles, and hardships, James points to the apocalyptic hope—the exaltation after the day of parousia.[19]

Was the letter designated to address both Jewish and gentile Christians? Painter outlines three major approaches for interpreting such an address: it referred to either "all believers, Jews and Gentiles," or "all Jews of the diaspora," or "all believing Jews of the diaspora," concluding that, "the epistle, like the mission "of the historical James, was oriented to the Jewish people."[20] The case is strong for seeing James effectively addressed to believing Jews of the diaspora. However, as Maynard-Reid states, "we must be careful not to say that James is addressing only Jewish Christians and that he is excluding the non-Christian Jews of the community." He continues, "this distinction between Christians and non-Christians may be artificial."[21]

15. Maynard-Reid, *Poverty and Wealth in James,* 13–14, 18.

16. Brosend, *James and Jude,* 31–32.

17. Theissen, *Social Reality and the Early Christians,* 246.

18. Witherington, *Jesus the Sage,* 246.

19. Perdue, "Paraenesis and the Epistle of James," 252.

20. Painter, "James as the First Catholic Epistle," 247–48.

21. Maynard-Reid, *Poverty and Wealth,* 10.

CHAPTER 1

James 1:1–27

IN CHAPTER 1, JAMES encouraged his readers going through various kinds of trials. Their attitude matters. The letter opens with an invitation to the readers to wrestle with the paradox of rejoicing in affliction. The author assumes that trials are very much part of Christian life and come in various forms. They are to remain joyful despite their circumstances. God will grant them wisdom to endure whatever trials come their way. He gives the community an assurance that will be a reward for overcomers. He also warns them against yielding to temptations. James taught that even when there are trials and tribulations in life, one should remain faithful. According to James, this test of faith is what builds tenacity. Verses 5–8 revolve around the two concepts of wisdom and double-mindedness, which he later addresses in 3:13–18 and 4.8, respectively. Both are important to James. He shows the interrelatedness of the two: the gift of wisdom is granted to those who trust in God, who are not double-minded. James implies that those who compromise their faith and look to the world and God for their security lack the essence of faith.

James hints at the problem of the poor and the rich in 1:9–11, a theme which he expands on at various points in the letter (2:2–4, 5–12; 4:13–17; 5:1–6). That the situation of the poor Christians is high on James's agenda is evident in the fact that it appears so early in the letter. James addresses various topics in 1:12–27, first addressing the problem of trials (12–15) that he first mentioned in 1:2–4. He does not only distinguish between temptations and trials but makes it clear that believers can be overcomers, assured of a reward from God. This is followed by a warning to his audience to avoid being deceived (16–18); exhortations concerning prudence in speech (19–21); hearing and "doing" (obeying) the word, and the essence of true religion (26–27).

VERSE 1

James, a bondservant of God and of the Lord Jesus Christ,
To the twelve tribes who are dispersed abroad: Greetings.

James begins the letter in standard ancient letter form by mentioning his name, the intended recipients, and short greetings. He does not indicate who he is or his status in the community. Instead, he modestly designates himself as a bondservant of God and of the Lord Jesus Christ. Although translated here as a bondservant (NASB), the ordinary meaning of the word *doulos* is a slave, which, though it was a term familiar term in the ancient world, is repulsive to common African readers of James. Today, the word is used in connection with oppression. The mention of slavery in Africa evokes mixed feelings and rightly so, particularly when one thinks of the cruelty, forced submission, and maltreatment that accompanied slavery. The challenge of what the word means to an African reader is clear in the word's translation in several African languages. For example, the word has different meanings in three major Nigerian languages. The Yoruba translate it as "*iranse*" (messenger); the Hausa translate it as "*bawan*" (slave), and the Igbo as "*orù*" (servant). In Swahili, a widely spoken language in East Africa, it is translated as "*ntumwa*" (slave), a word that is also multivalent. It includes such meanings as an agent, one that is sent, or property of another. Bishop Samuel Ajayi Crowther, a freed slave who later became the first Anglican bishop in Africa and was a linguist, and did the first translation of the Bible in the Yoruba language, translated the word *doulos* as "servant" instead of its ordinary meaning "slave." It makes one to wonder how much the influence of his own experience on his choice of the word was. The word *iranse* has many nuances with profound implications for the Christian life. It is synonymous with "messenger" and we can also understand it as *omo odo*, an apprentice. Understood in the former sense, an African reader would see James as an emissary of Christ. Therefore, his words carry much authority. In the latter sense, James, although an apostle, is a continuous learner or a disciple. The church must recognize that discipleship is a continuous following of Christ, rather than a six- to eight-week program of discipleship training. We never stop being disciples regardless of the position we occupy in the church. Regardless of which James might have written the letter, his self-designation as a slave or servant is very instructive. For James, being a slave of God and Christ differs from that of an ordinary African reader. An ordinary servant, in the normal sense of the word, provides his or her services to anyone who pays well, and feels at liberty to change his/her employer, if such change is advantageous. But a slave is the property of the master; he/she belongs to the master and is not at liberty to leave the master; even any property that the slave acquires belongs to the master. It is a self-effacing word that James applies to himself. It is a voluntary submission to the will of God. There is no hint of forced submission or coercion. Although not coerced, obedience is also required, something that is implied in James's exhortation to his audience to be doers of the word. The history of Christianity in Africa suggests otherwise. In most cases, Christianization of Africa was in the context of the slave trade with its attending oppression. Christianity was one justification that the European powers used to colonize and exploit Africa.

In sum, we may suggest that James's introduction is probably connected with his overall rhetorical strategy of downplaying one's social or economic status, something that resonates throughout the entire book. James's introductory salutation should remind modern church leaders, especially in Africa, of the need to be sober and to recognize their limitation as servants of the Lord. His style is a strong rebuke to many church leaders who play God, and it also undermines the arrogance of church leaders who surround themselves with so many bodyguards that line up in front and behind and sometimes beside them when they are walking to the preaching podium or pulpit! James's introduction is a not-so-subtle rebuke to the common notion of "Africa's Big Men" who personalize power and use repression and manipulation to hang on to power. For example, it is not only uncommon but also it is a shame to see a fellow pastor venting his anger at his driver when the latter failed to open the pastor's car door for him or when he did not carry the "senior pastor's" briefcase in front of him. I remember an incident where a pastor chided his fellow pastor for allowing the driver to sit in the back seat (usually known as owner's corner) with him.

James designates his addressees as 'the twelve tribes dispersed abroad,' a designation that is rather ambiguous. Literally, he calls them the twelve tribes in the diaspora. The term suggests that they lived in these areas as aliens and sojourners.[1] It is probably right to suggest that he does so to stress their social condition as "outcasts" (cf. Ps 147:2, LXX 146:2).[2] The

---

1. Serrão, James, 47.

2. The question of the exile and the self-understanding of the Jews in the Greco-Roman period is a complex one and remains unresolved, with two diametrically opposed scholarly views dominating the conversation. On the one hand are scholars who understand the experience of the exiles as negative and on the other hand are those who see the experience as positive. In the former case, it is argued that the diaspora Jews of the Greco-Roman period saw the situation as resulting from divine punishment in accordance with the covenant curses in Leviticus 26 and Deuteronomy 28. In that case the negative concept of living outside the land (one of the boundary markers for the Jews) was not transformed into a positive concept. Thomas Kraabel, a representative of

same word appears in 2 Macc. 1:27 where it refers to the forsaken and re- jected: "Gather together our scattered people, set free those who are slaves among the Gentiles, look on those who are rejected and despised, and let the Gentiles know that you are our God." It is easy to imagine that the ad- dressees were not living comfortably but were people who were away from their original homeland and whose identity is at the risk of being eroded. The believers to whom James wrote are scattered all over the Roman Empire (and perhaps beyond, as there was a large Jewish community in Babylonia/ Parthia) and viewed with suspicion and perhaps with open hostility. Some of the scattered Jewish Christians may have been born where they lived. But from a sociological perspective, their ethnic and religious background distinguished them from those who lived around them. Their values and lifestyle differed from those of the cities they inhabited. They were open to ridicule, perhaps even physical and social abuse, for their beliefs and prac- tices.[3] Therefore, they are called exiles. Although she might have enjoyed the comfort or protection of Mr. Tulliver, Maggie's feeling of exile is well summed up by George Elliot.[4] She writes:

> There is no sense of ease like the ease we felt in those scenes where we were born, where objects became dear to us before we had known the labour of choice, and where the outer world seemed only an extension of our own personality.[5]

To be in exile is to be in a discontinuous state of being cut off form one's roots, land, and past. One is never at home in exile, however comfort- able the situation may be. Exile is a place of loneliness, non-belonging. The psalmist aptly describes the situation of an exile:

> By the rivers of Babylon,
> There we sat down and wept,
> When we remembered Zion.
> Upon the willows in the midst of it
> We hung our harps.
> For there our captors demanded of us songs,

---

the latter view, suggests that the originally negative concept of exile was gradually trans- formed into a positive concept. Although an African in diaspora, "an exile by choice," I can attest to the fact that the two conditions are not mutually exclusive. Being in the diaspora could be a place of inclusion and exclusion, comfort and confusion, both at the same time.

3. Serrão, *James*, 48.

4. George Eliot is the pen name of Mary Anne Evans, an English novelist, poet, journalist, translator, and one of the leading writers of the Victorian era.

5. Eliot, *Mill on the Floss*, 119.

And our tormentors mirth, *saying,*
"Sing us one of the songs of Zion."
How can we sing the LORD's song
In a foreign land?
If I forget you, O Jerusalem,
May my right hand forget *her skill.*
May my tongue cling to the roof of my mouth
If I do not remember you,
If I do not exalt Jerusalem
Above my chief joy.
Remember, O LORD, against the sons of Edom
The day of Jerusalem,
Who said, "Raze it, raze it
To its very foundation."
O daughter of Babylon, you devastated one,
How blessed will be the one who repays you
With the recompense with which you have repaid us.
How blessed will be the one who seizes and dashes your little ones
Against the rock.

The readers may ask in what sense the foregoing applies to Africans on the continent, African Americans, and Africans in the diaspora.[6] The psalmist's cry mirrors that of Africans today as they struggle to make sense of the devastation, ravaging of wars, economic deprivation, and various ills that plague the continent. In highlighting one problem of exiles, Joel Green succinctly states:

> . . . exile is a time of temptation and testing. . . . The experience of the exile resides in the social and religious threat confronting a people challenged with the perennial possibility and threat of assimilation and defection. James refers to this as the problem of *peirasmos*—a Greek term that can be translated as 'testing' and 'temptation'. The paradox which we find in James and 1 Peter, is that the very process that can lead to growth in

6. Harris, *Africans and Their History,* passim, defined the African diaspora as the voluntary and involuntary dispersion of Africans globally throughout history; the emergence of a cultural identity based on origin and social condition; and the psychological and physical return of those in the diaspora to Africa. Within this definition, Africa is clearly based at the center of any discussion of the diaspora and has created a tenuous debate within both scholarly and popular circles as to whether the diaspora remains connected directly to Africa as evidenced by the numerous Africanisms and cultural retentions in the diaspora that demonstrate to some an unyielding linkage between Africa and the diaspora unaffected by slavery, or is the diaspora something else, with its members impacted as much by the social, cultural, and economic legacies of slavery and colonialism in the Americas as by their ancestral homes on the African continent.

faith and faithfulness towards God (that is, 'testing') can also lead to the loss of faithfulness, even falling away from faith (that, is 'temptation').[7]

One could hear the echoes of the psalm in the lyrics of the song of Nigerians that were sold into slavery on their way to an uncertain future and unknown destination:

> *By the bank of Niger River,*
> *we slept in the night when the moonlight so bright;*
> *by the banks of Niger River.*
> *I have no father in this town,*
> *I have no mother in this town;*
> *We slept in the night when the moonlight so bright;*
> *By the banks of Niger River.*

Presently, Nigeria, the largest and most populous country in Africa, is under siege on various levels. The economy is in shambles; religious intolerance is on the rise; there are thousands of internally displaced persons (outcasts or exiles), mainly Christians with little or no hope for the future. The same is true of Sudan, Gambia, and other countries. The rich are getting richer and the poor, poorer. There is insecurity and Christians are afraid of being overrun by Muslims. There is perhaps no better time than now to hear and heed the words of James. In depicting the social situation of his audience as "exiles," James shows that it is possible to be an exile even in one's own land. In post-independence Africa, various tensions and conflicts exist in many countries. These often escalated into internecine strife and civil wars or wars between states, with the consequent destruction of human lives and entire societies. The reasons for these conflicts go back to the fact that the colonial powers had arbitrarily drawn boundaries, like those of Nigeria, amalgamating people of different cultures or separating people of the same culture. In its report issued on May 10, 2019, the Internal Displacement Monitoring Centre of the Norwegian Refugee Centre reports that the countries in sub-Saharan Africa experienced more internal displacement than any other region in 2018. According to the report, "unresolved and cyclical conflict combined with new waves of violence to trigger 7.4 million displacements between January and December 2018, an increase on 2017 and three times more than in the Middle East and North Africa."[8]

---

7. Green, *Reading Scripture as Wesleyans*, 120–21.

8. Internal Displacement Monitoring Centre, "10 Million People Internally Displaced Across Sub-Saharan Africa in 2018."

VERSES 2–4

Consider it all joy, my brethren, when you encounter various trials,
knowing that the testing of your faith produces endurance.
And let endurance have its perfect result, so that you may be perfect and com-
plete, lacking in nothing.

James seeks to encourage and comfort his readers in their "various trials" which they will have to endure by assuring them that these very troubles may become the means by which they may become mature in their faith. Now he addresses them as brethren (the Greek plural *adelphoi* can refer to a mixed group of brothers and sisters), a familial term that he uses in several places in the letter.[9] James immediately begins to address the situation of his addresses—they were going through times of trials and difficulties.[10] However, James does not get into the specifics of the nature of the trials that his audience faced. That trials are part of life is an accepted fact by everyone, more so by a typical African whose life is mired in suffering, sometimes from birth to death. Trials come in different forms and shapes.[11] For James, Christianity does not insulate one or offer a refuge from the arrows and darts of adversity. Persecution was the most common trial among the followers of Christ in James's time. According to a new Pew Research Center report, there are already more Christians in Africa than any other continent. By 2060, six of the ten countries with the largest Christian populations will be in Africa, up from three in 2015.[12] But as Christianity grows in Africa, so does the persecution of Christians. Christians are increasingly seen as a threat to Muslim-dominated lands and governments. The northern part of Nigeria is a case in point. Conversion to Christianity is like signing one's

9. 1:16, 19; 2:1, 5, 14; 3:1, 10, 12; 4:22, 57, 9, 10, 12, 19. The importance of this word for the motif of Christian discipleship is well-discussed by Peter H. Davids who highlights the significance of the community as the context of discipleship. See David, "Controlling the Tongue and the Wallet," 225–47.

10. "The Greek word *peirasmos* can be translated either as "trial" or as "temptation," and the second of these possibilities dominated the Fathers' interpretation of these verses. To them the cure for temptation was patient endurance, which was the fruit of a spiritual wisdom that could be obtained only from God. There was no problem with obtaining this, as long as believers asked God for wisdom in faith, without doubting that they would receive it" (Bray, *James, 1–2 Peter, 1–3, John, Jude*, 4). The present context suggests a wider meaning than temptations.

11. Various translates the Greek word *poikilos* which means "variegated," "all kinds of," or "different kinds of." In the present context it means "all the various sorts of troubles" that test human life, particularly as Christians, "of whatever kind they may be."

12. McClendon, "Sub-Saharan Africa Will Be Home."

death warrant. Muslim parents sometimes kill their children who convert to following Christ. A Kenyan pastor told the story of several Massai women who were publicly tortured by their unsaved husbands and family members. The reason was because they refused to participate in the immoral cultural practice of allowing their husbands' peers to have sexual relations with them. Despite all the sufferings, they stood firm in their faith and, today, they are heroines of faith among the Massai believers.

Apart from persecution, today's world offers many kinds of trial: the loss of a family member, failed business, the loss of a job, a divorce, trouble with our children, severe financial strain, illness or death in the family, or relational problems over which we seem to have little control. Although our present trials may differ from those of James's day, the nature of which James does not elaborate, he nevertheless offers some practical advice of what to do not "if" we encounter trials, but "when" we encounter trials. And when these trials come, our first strategy, according to James, is to "consider it all joy."

James's exhortation brings into mind African resilience. "Consider it all joy" is James's admonition to Christians when going through trials and difficult times. The Greek form of the word rendered "consider" implies a decisive choice concerning one's mindset rather than a passive attitude of mind or fatal resignation. It does not suggest a rationalization but a thinking ahead to the outcome of the trial, rather than focus on the immediate or present crushing circumstances as if the troubles will not end. Definitely, James is not suggesting or insinuating that believers should resign to fate or just go about laughing when troubles come. Rather he is calling for spiritual reflection when trials come, and mentions joy, an important aspect of the fruit of the Spirit that Paul mentions in Gal 5:22–23. James encourages his readers not to despair because of their trials but, rather to bear up under them, relying on God, recognizing that he is using their trials for their good. People have often wondered why despite all its economic, social, and political problems Africans remain resilient. As noted by Dahir:

> Africa, home to 16% of the world's population, is the unhappiest continent. The continent featured at the bottom of the list of the World Happiness Report, a survey released this month that ranks global happiness in 155 countries. People in the 44 African countries surveyed faced 'happiness deficit' because they scored low in key indicators that lead to well-being and happiness such as freedom, good governance, health provision and income equality. However, enduring poverty or living under authoritarian rule doesn't necessarily translate to espousing a grim view of the future. As the Africa chapter of the report notes, Africans showed "exceptional" global levels of optimism

and resilience to their less-than-perfect circumstances. The optimism was underwritten by the coping mechanisms developed
over decades of dealing with poor infrastructure; lack of water,
food, and electricity; and poor living standards. Africans also
found comfort in their different systems of faith and worship.
Having faith in God keeps many people in suffering hopeful that
things will become better.[13]

James's admonition brings to the fore the negative effects of the so-
called "prosperity gospel" in Africa. One major question that needs to be
addressed more adequately concerns the preaching of the "prosperity gospel" in Africa in recent years and its response to suffering, sickness, and
poverty among believers. It is a question to which James may provide an answer in 1:2–4. Should one ever conclude as some of the "prosperity gospel"
preachers do, that believers who go through these problems are less than
Christians or spiritually deficient? James would respond with a resounding
"No." As James would later argue in 1:9–11, it is indeed possible for a believer to be of low circumstances. Sociologically, the view of wealth as blessing
and sign of faith or lack of it could easily become a spiritual justification for
contempt for the poor who are seen the cause of their own poverty.

Africa's optimism may be exceptional. African people demonstrate in-
genuity that makes life bearable even under intolerable circumstances. Re-
counting her own experience and affirming an opinion that first appeared in
the British newspaper *The Guardian* on January 11, 2011, Bim Adewunmi, a
Nigerian-born British citizen, affirms the description of Nigeria as the happiest place on earth. She writes:

> Daily life is hardly one glorious Technicolor dance sequence,
> but I have never lived in such a happy place—and I once lived
> in hippyville California. I can't give a definite answer, but I think
> the joy comes from seeing and living through the worst that life
> can offer; it is an optimism born of hope. Nigeria is a nation of
> Del Boy Trotters ("this time next year, we'll be millionaires!")—
> while the rest of the world believes they've got a book in them,
> most Nigerians believe they've got a million quid in them, too.
>
> I am living proof of this: in the years I lived and learned
> in Lagos, I saw some pretty awful stuff—the state-sanctioned
> execution of freedom fighter and environmentalist Ken Saro-
> Wiwa, the military rule of the IBB era, the annulment of the
> democratic 12 June elections to name but a few—and managed
> to come out the other side laughing. And why shouldn't we
> laugh? We are firm believers in the New Labour theme tune:

13. Dahir, "Joy in Happiness."

things can only get better. There's a Yoruba saying that my father often uses: "Jimoh toma l'oyin, Alamisi le yan ma ti mo." It translates roughly as: "If a Friday is to be sweet, you'll know by Thursday." It might not seem like Nigerians have much to be happy about, but perhaps they've already seen what Friday holds, and what they see makes them rejoice.[14]

Adewunmi's point may be summed up by the saying that when there is life, there is hope. The story below further sheds light on African optimism in the midst of trials.

Why I Can Sing

Moro Naba, a Mossi emperor in Burkina Faso, had conquered a powerful ethnic group in the south called the Kasena. He extracted tribute from them once each year.

One year, at tribute collecting time, the emperor made the mistake of sending his son Nabiiga, a prince and his heir apparent. When the Kasena saw him with only a very small entourage of guardians, they overpowered the group and took the prince hostage.

His kingly robes were stripped from him and he was forced to walk around in only a loincloth. The prisoner received only one meal a day and was forced out into the fields each morning to hoe. Normally, manual labor would be beneath the dignity of a royal heir, so the Kasena made great sport of him. The women would pass by and belittle his manhood. While he was hoeing in the fields, the children would throw pebbles and stones at him.

But, to the surprise of all those watching from day to day, the Mossi prince would work and sing. He sang cheerfully with a loud voice as his back bent to the hoe from sunup to sundown. At first his soft hands blistered and then bled as he was unaccustomed to using a hoe. He lost much weight, but continued to be cheerful and to sing.

The elders of the Kasena were much troubled by his singing and buoyant attitude. "How can he possibly sing," they would ask, "since we make him sleep on the ground? We give him very little food and he is forced to work. Our women and children mock him, but he still sings!"

After a month of watching, they finally called him before a council. He stood in his loincloth, straight and proud in their midst. The elder spokesperson for the Kasena people asked the Mossi prince about this behavior, "Why do you sing?"

14. Adewunmi, "Nigeria."

Nabiiga answered, "It is true. You have taken away my fine clothes. You have made me work, you give me very little food and you make me sleep on the ground in a common hut. You have tried to take away all my pride and all my earthly possessions. You have brought me great shame. Now you ask me why in spite of all this, I can sing. I sing because you cannot take away my title and who I am. I am Moro Naba's first son and need not react to your shameful behavior!"[15]

What kept Nabiiga going? It was his sense of identity. Like Nabiiga, the African readers of James live in the reality of their knowledge of who God is and of their relationship to him. James consistently bases his expectation of the kind of life that is to characterize his readers on his understanding of the nature of God (shaping his readers' understanding of the same, by implication). Christians are to live, James argues, in full consciousness of the character of the God they serve. Thus, it is because God gives "generously and without reproach" that Christians should not hesitate to ask him for wisdom (1:5). James emphasizes the goodness of God's gifts in 1:17 and also stresses the invariability of God's character. God gives everything that is perfect, James asserts, and is incapable of being enticed by evil. Because of this, James's readers were not to think that God would ever be the author of their temptation (1:13). In sum, to "count," or "consider" it all joy in the midst of our trials is to respond with a deliberate, intelligent appraisal of our situation. We must learn to look at our situation from God's perspective and recognize that, though the trial is not a happy experience in itself, it is God's way of producing something of great value. James is not saying we are to rejoice over pain, but we are to rejoice because God's purposes are being accomplished in our lives. As hard as it may seem to the ears, James encourages the believers to know that the trial of their faith serves a purpose—it produces endurance. Scholars agree that religion permeates every dimension of African life. Africans look up to God in every circumstance and see him as the supreme center, who, despite what we are going through, is the "ultimate explanation of the genesis and sustenance of both man and all things."[16]

Verses 3–4 show that trials should be the means of growth in the believer's faith. Christians should profit from trials not by asking "why did it happen" but "what does God's word say in this situation?" In verse 4, James uses the term *perfection* for the first time. That this term is significant for James is not only to be noted by the number of its occurrences in this short

---

15. Tarr, *Double Image*, 69.

16. Mbiti, *African Religion and Philosophy*, 20.

letter but also in its placement (twice in 1:14 and 1:17 and 1:25). He uses the verb to make perfect or complete in 2:22 and the verb to fulfill or accomplish in 2:8. There are two important questions to be answered. First, what does "perfection" mean for James? Second, how does the African understanding of perfection enhance James's quest for perfection? With regard to the former, the starting point is to note that, for James, perfection is a goal. With regard to the latter, the ways in which the words "perfect," "complete," and "lacking nothing" offer some clues. E níláti ní ìfaradà tìtí dé òpin, kí ẹ lè di pípé, kí ẹ sì ní ohun gbogbo lekunrẹ́rẹ́, láìsí ikùnà kankan. It translates as: "You must persevere till the end in order to be perfect (pípé), complete or full to the brim (lekunrẹ́rẹ́), without failure or blemish (láìsí ikùnà kankan)." The other word used here means "full to the brim" and it further explains the phrase "without failure or blemish," thus suggesting that the words teleioi (perfect) and holoklēros (complete) have ethical/moral content in Yoruba tradition. Notably, the adjective holoklēros (complete) appears only here and in 1 Thess 5:23 within Paul's prayer for the entire sanctification of his readers. There the emphasis is on the preservation of the whole (holoklēron) person—"spirit, soul and body"—blameless before God.[17] It is an understanding of perfection that is dynamic. "Maturity does not just develop over time. Only divine cultivation effects the kind of physical, spiritual, and mental wholeness James expects. He is concerned about the entire character of the Christian."[18]

VERSES 5–8

But if any of you lacks wisdom, let him ask of God, who gives to all generously and without reproach, and it will be given to him.
But he must ask in faith without any doubting, for the one who doubts is like the surf of the sea, driven and tossed by the wind.
For that man ought not to expect that he will receive anything from the Lord, being a double-minded man, unstable in all his ways.

Wisdom occupies an important place in Jewish literature and James has often been considered as belonging to that genre. At the beginning of his exhortation to his readers who lived in a foreign environment, James urges them to ask for wisdom from God, suggesting a second step of handling trial—praying for wisdom. James stands fully with Israel's wisdom tradition:

17. Serrão, *James*, 52.
18. Serrão, *James*, 52.

> The fear of the Lord is the beginning of wisdom, but fools despise wisdom and discipline. (Prov 1:7)

> For the Lord gives wisdom, and from his mouth come knowledge and understanding. (Prov 2:6)

Wisdom will enable the believers to understand God's ways and how to approach life in a proper manner despite their circumstances. A Yoruba maxim goes, *Ogbon l'afi ngbe aye*, that is, "One needs wisdom to live in this world." The main idea is that wisdom is indispensable. Trials can destabilize even the most sophisticated person. Confusion, frustration, and lack of focus can be exhibited by anyone facing trials or problems. James knows this can happen to Christians as they face difficulties in life. Lest James's audience get discouraged, he is quick to assure them that they are not left on their own. So, he urged them to pray for wisdom from God. This wisdom here is the discipline of applying truth to one's life in the light of experience. Wisdom is not simply intellectual knowledge that can be acquired in a classroom, nor is it mere philosophical speculation. It is spiritual understanding and knowledge that comes from God through his revealed word. It is essential to making daily choices and life-changing decisions well.

James offers a simple lesson in prayer here. Rather than going through frustration, worrying, and giving others around us serious concerns, we should go to the Lord in prayer. The Lord works wonders through prayer in such situations. The lesson here is that we have a God who is our Refuge, the great Shelter, and One who specializes in solving problems. When Solomon, the young, inexperienced new king of Israel was beginning to experience the trial of leading a great nation, he sought the face of God for wisdom and the Lord gave it to him in abundance (1 Kgs 3:6–12). Prayer in times of trial enables us to acknowledge before God that we are inadequate, that we are helpless, and that he alone can help us in our time of need. We are told to pray without doubting. We should not be restless like the waves of the sea, that is, we should be stable and settled before God alone, without wavering back and forth between two or three opinions. He gave wisdom to Solomon so liberally, and he is capable of giving us the same wisdom without holding back. James is bragging about our generous God who is liberal to those who put their trust in him. The adverb translated "generously"(*haplōs*) can mean "*simply, . . . sincerely, openly*."[19] It occurs only here in the New Testament. The translation *who gives sincerely to all* is also possible. That James follows this appeal by insisting that his readers must "ask in faith, never doubting" (v. 6 NRSV) suggests *sincerely* as a possible option. But the verb *gives* favors

19. Bauer and Danker, *Green-English Lexicon*, 104.

generously as the better translation. In Rom 12:8 and 2 Cor 8:2, 9:11, and 13 the cognate abstract noun *haplotēs* means "generosity" or "liberality" (NASB).[20] We should therefore have confidence in God, and never entertain any doubt about his willingness to give us the wisdom we ask of him.

James says that a double-souled person cannot please the God or expect to receive anything from him. This verse is both an encouragement and a warning to the African reader in a special way. The suffering believer is encouraged to trust in God in terms of trouble. As a warning, it exposes the danger of syncretism and the notion that "*Olorun o kaajo*," which means that God is not averse to people helping themselves. That is explicit in the adage, "*eniti o ba ran ara re lowo ni Olorun nran l'owo*," which translates as the familiar "God helps those who help themselves." In an African pragmatic way this speaks of those who engage in syncretism, who in times of need turn back to seek help from native diviners, mystical powers, or ancestral spirits. In the context of persecuted Christians in Africa, this passage urges steadfastness and unflinching commitment to Christ in the face of adversities. There are to be none of the divided loyalties and divided affections that characterize people with "soft commitment" who are easily blown away by the external forces *of their surrounding culture or cave at the slightest trial of their faith.*

VERSES 9–11

But the brother of humble circumstances is to glory in his high position;
and the rich man is to glory in his humiliation, because like flowering grass he will pass away.
For the sun rises with a scorching wind and withers the grass; and its flower falls off and the beauty of its appearance is destroyed; so too the rich man in the midst of his pursuits will fade away.

The social context of this section is similar to that which predominates that of the majority world today, especially the African continent—one in which the poor have little power and are easily taken advantage of by the rich and powerful in society. Many of James's readers were probably poor foreigners and immigrants. Poverty and riches can become trials or test for anyone. There are "prosperity gospel" preachers in Africa who do not know what to do with a phrase like "the brother in humble circumstances" because for them if a person is a Christian, then he or she can never be in "humble

20. Serrão, *James*, 54.

circumstances" for long. He or she is only there because he/she does not have enough faith to name and claim riches. Poverty has led many people to engage in many evils, such as stealing or armed robbery. Some have even looked for ways to commit suicide, because they just cannot stand being out of money, or because they are ashamed that they are unable to live like their neighbors who are considered rich, though the neighbors may not necessarily be rich at all. Although James does not promote poverty, he nevertheless shows that it is possible to be a Christian and be poor, something which is the reality of many African Christians. There are potential dangers facing poor people. Poverty is not a safe place to be. The poor Christians, James suggests, are not to be despondent but rather should rejoice in their relationship with God despite their circumstances. They must put their lives in proper perspective as James presents a contrast to the rich people whose riches are only temporal. On the other hand, riches have led many people to abandon the Source of the wealth and made the money their God or idol. A typical example is the rich young ruler in Luke 18:18–30. The most shocking statement of our Lord concerning riches is the problem the rich people face, that is, it is hard or difficult for wealthy people to enter the kingdom of heaven (cf. Luke 18:24). Of course, the Lord means those who are busy piling up riches for themselves above love for their neighbor in need. Another example is the man who had abundance of harvest and who decided to hoard the harvest for his own selfish use. In his own case, wealth became a source of trial, but he failed the test (Luke 12:11–15).

Wealth in modern times can create all kinds of trials. Solomon Ishola tells the story of four girls in Nigeria who came from rich homes and who were very promising but became greedy and were unsatisfied. They formed a gang, and were robbing neighborhood stores at gunpoint. They used masks anytime they were going for their robbery raid, and they did it several times but they were eventually caught. The top lawyers that were secured by their parents were unable to get them free from being jailed for seven years each. The gang leader was just sixteen years of age, and she was given seven and a half years! In spite of wealth and so-called mansions in which they were living, they became miscreants.

Several years ago, one of the wealthiest men in Nigeria at that time slumped and died during a flight. His burial was attended by the "Who's Who" of Nigeria. Several months after his burial two friends were overheard talking about the elaborate funeral ceremony. In the course of the conversation one of the friends said something to the effect that "with all that man's money, he was not buried inside the church building." He was buried in the same burial ground where the poorest member of the community was buried. His riches did not make a difference. It offers a lesson to both the poor and the rich to avoid the temptation that either having or not having wealth brings.

VERSES 12–15

Blessed is a man who perseveres under trial; for once he has been approved, he will receive the crown of life which the Lord has promised to those who love Him.

Let no one say when he is tempted, "I am being tempted by God"; for God cannot be tempted by evil, and He Himself does not tempt anyone.

But each one is tempted when he is carried away and enticed by his own lust. Then when lust has conceived, it gives birth to sin; and when sin is accomplished, it brings forth death.

James takes up again the theme of trials that he first mentioned in 1:2–4. It is notable that James uses the word *peirasmos* for "trial." The word carries double meaning: (i) an ordeal of suffering or distress and strain; (ii) an enticement or temptation to do evil. As such, the meaning is to be determined by the context. This is the case in verses 12–15, where the two usages are present. In verse 12, the first of the two meanings predominates. James encourages believers to persevere in trials and counts those who endure as blessed (cf. Matt 5:11–12).

Although there is no allusion to social, racial, or gender equality in the text,[21] the promise and possibility of a crown of life to all overcomers is especially liberating for an African reader of James at all levels. First, in the midst of prevalent social injustice and equality, the ordinary African Christian has something to look forward to. Second is the hope that the text offers to African women who, in mostly patriarchal communities across the continent, are excluded from high positions in life. Although African history has detailed a few cases where women not only participated but led and won in wars, they are rarely mentioned or celebrated.[22] He does not only provide encouragement for women who are undergoing persecution and trials at the moment but offers an eschatological hope. As overcomers they will wear the crown of life. Here they can truly sing the song as victorious followers of the Lamb; they can truly wear the crown when the battle is over.

21. See Painter and deSilva, *James and Jude*, 66 on the use of use *anēr* and *anthropos* in the letter of James.

22. For some examples, see Achebe, *Female Monarchs and Merchant Queens in Africa*.

James's assertion that God does not tempt anyone naturally prompted the question about the African view of causality. It is interesting to note that the words "tempt" and "test/try" are translated with the same word *idanwo* in the Yoruba Bible. As such the Yoruba reader makes a decision based on the context, opting for the former in verse 12 and the latter in verse 13. For Africans, "the inter-relatedness of causes between the supernatural world and the natural world is borne out of the belief that the world is a unitary whole where the spiritual coalesces with the physical."[23] Carried to an extreme, one may come to the erroneous conclusion of "the devil made me do it" and in this case "God made me do it." James would have none of such ideas but placed the responsibility squarely on the individual.

VERSES 16-18

Do not be deceived, my beloved brethren.
Every good thing given and every perfect gift is from above, coming down from the Father of lights, with whom there is no variation or shifting shadow.
In the exercise of His will He brought us forth by the word of truth, so that we would be a kind of first fruits among His creatures.

James's warning (v. 16) to his readers to avoid being deceived is significant. It serves as a warning to those who might resort to blaming God for falling prey to their own temptation in light of the nature and character of God (vv. 17-18). Verse 16 also further reiterates and underlines the danger of doubting the generosity and goodness of God that he mentioned earlier in 1:6-7. Such doubt leads to being unable to receive the answer to one's petition from God (1:8), whom James now portrays as the good, unchanging Father (1:17). James's portrayal of God as an unchanging Father is very much at home within the African context where God is seen as the first and ultimate cause of things. Writing about the unchanging character of God as an African, Metuh underscores the fact that God "is constant and does not change from good to bad and vice versa according to the situation. The fact that he is above petty influences and does what only himself wants . . . makes his character primarily good."[24] In Africa, God is experienced as the good parent, a source of loving-kindness and protection. Human beings

---

23. Akpan, "Comparative Analysis," 722.
24. Tanner, *Transition in African Belief,* 7.

experience closeness to God, which they describe in terms of motherhood and fatherhood.[25]

Writing about the African experience of God, Magesa rightly states:

> The relationship between God and creation—specifically humanity—is one of solicitude on the part of God. To associate God with anything that is not good, pure, just and honorable is ridiculous. The expression "It is God's will," uttered when Africans experience difficulties from which they cannot escape delineates this belief. People know that misfortune can happen, but they believe that it is always with the knowledge or permission of God, yet . . . God is never blamed for this; instead the ultimate source of misfortune and suffering is to be found in the created order.[26]

The challenge was always to discern God at work. Does God take sides? If so, whose side is God on, and why? The African experience of God is that ultimately God is on the side of the weak and the side of justice. James also presents the picture of a heavenly father who is trustworthy, the unchangeable one that is intimately involved, emotional, and compassionate. James sees God as the good and generous giver (1:5–8, 17–18, 21), attributes that make the ungenerous faith in 2:14–17 all the more shocking. The lack of generosity toward the hungry and needy on the part of those who have experienced God's generosity themselves calls into question their faith in this God. Knowing this God is what makes it possible to endure the trials of life as occasions of joy. This is the theological foundation of true religion. James's words here recall the words of Jeremiah in the book of Lamentations: "Because of the LORD's great love we are not consumed, for his compassions never fail. They are new every morning; great is your faithfulness" (Lam 3:22–23). When the prophet Jeremiah wrote those words, he was surrounded by the desolation of a captive and destroyed Jerusalem. Outwardly there was no reason to have such hope. All the circumstances of the prophet's life at that moment would belie such hopefulness.[27]

Having warned the audience not to be misled about God's character, James proceeds to make that character apparent. He begins with the statement: "Every generous act of giving, with every perfect gift, is from above, coming down . . ." (1:17). The redundancy within this statement

---

25. Although James calls God "Father," one must note that the image of God in African societies is not always patriarchal. See, for example, Taringa, "African Metaphors," 174–79.

26. Magesa, *African Religion*, 41. See also Metuh, *God and Man*, 43.

27. Walters, *James*, 53–55.

highlights the extravagant generosity of God, from whom good gifts keep coming. These gifts are not the same as the outcome of endurance in 1:12 (the "crown of life" to be awarded), but the sum total of every good aspect of life that cannot be earned, such as wisdom (1:5) and redemption (1:18). In contrast, to those who sought to argue that God could be both the source of good gifts and yet also responsible for temptation, James adds that in this God "there is no variation or shadow due to change." God consistently seeks to give his people the good things that they need so that they can live lives marked by God's consistency and generosity.

VERSE 19–21

This you know, my beloved brethren. But everyone must be quick to hear, slow to speak and slow to anger;
for the anger of man does not achieve the righteousness of God.
Therefore, putting aside all filthiness and all that remains of wickedness, in humility receive the implanted word, which is able to save your souls.

James's exhortation to his audience to be quick to hear and slow to speak can be well expressed by the Yoruba proverb *"Eyin l'oro; bo ba ba'le fifo ni nfo"* ("Words are raw eggs; when they drop on the floor, they shatter into pieces"). The import of the proverb is that words are fragile; once spoken (broken), they cannot be retrieved. This statement well sums up James's admonition to his readers to be slow in speaking.

Ishola narrates an African story, meant to be humorous, about a woman who went to consult a diviner (*babalawo* as they are known) for help about her marital problems.[28] The *diviners*, in addition to predicting the future, also engage in healing and serve as traditional counselors on moral issues. The woman and the husband constantly quarreled without let up due to constant arguments and bickering. Because the woman always responded angrily to her husband, used abusive words, and shouted expletives, she became a punching bag; always severely beaten. The diviner being able to see through her problem gave her advice and gave her a small pebble to put in her mouth whenever an argument arises among them. She was strictly instructed to make sure that the pebble does not fall down from her mouth, otherwise, the medicine (contained in the pebble) would not work. To the woman's surprise it worked because whenever the husband talked angrily, she was quiet. Her mouth had to be shut because of the pebble. Eventually

28. Ishola, *Putting Faith to Work*, 27–28.

the husband also changed his attitude because it had become useless to pick a fight with his now "quiet wife." The importance of the story lies in understanding what it means to be "quick to hear and slow to speak." One must be quick to add that the domestic abuse in this story does not agree with James's quest for social justice. It is obvious that both of them needed pebbles in their mouths—and he needed restraints on his arms!

James uses the term *"orgē"* for "anger" (1:19). It is a "state of relatively strong displeasure, with focus on the emotional aspect."[29] It can also imply a deeply settled inclination, as when New Testament texts employ it to refer to God's settled disposition toward sin and sinners—a righteous anger (John 3:36; Rom 1:18, 12:19; Eph 5:6; Col 3:6; 1 Thess 2:16; Heb 3:11, 4:3; Rev 11:18). But James specifically insists that human anger (*orgē*) does not produce or bring about righteousness. So, when James uses this term in reference to human beings, it is a uniformly negative word. Anger is a basic human emotion that, like all emotions, can be morally neutral. Wrath, on the other hand, speaks of a kind of *willful choice* on the part of the person involved. It is selfish. It is always counterproductive. The drive for retribution, even in understandable circumstances, is to be put into low gear, says James. Why? He offers one compelling reason: Human wrath does not produce the kind of life that God has purposed for us (1:20). Our lives are to be consistent responses to what God has willed, to what God has chosen. Anger, says James, cannot meet that standard; it cannot possibly bring about the kind of life God wills for his children.[30] It does not promote righteousness. Christians in today's world must realize that anger, retribution, and vindictiveness will not bring about or promote the kingdom of God which we claim to be seeking.

James spells out the implications of verses 19–20 with the instructions of verse 21: "Therefore, putting aside all filthiness and *all* that remains of wickedness, in humility receive the implanted word, which is able to save your souls." Using exceptionally blunt language, James urges his audience first, to get rid of "filthiness" or "impurity" (NEB: "all that is sordid"). It implies all moral filth, sordid avarice, and all that defiles in God's sight. The word James uses is found only here in the Greek New Testament. The African translation of the word as "dirt" or "pollution," which is essentially understood as a religious phenomenon, sheds some light on the verse in light of James's emphasis on the problems that can come with wealth (see 2:1–13, 5:1–6). The idea of ridding ourselves of impurity is notable, given James's insistence throughout the letter on purity, authenticity and single-mindedness

29. Bauer and Danker, *Greek-English Lexicon*, 720.
30. Walters, *James*, 61.

(versus double-mindedness). James includes "all that remains" of wickedness. In the present context, the word *perisseia*, although literally translated as "abundance," suggests that the Christians should get rid of and discard all forms of evil. James is appealing for an inner transformation that leads to outward change.

Second, this "ridding of" or "putting off" is to be accompanied by a corresponding "receiving" or "taking to oneself" the implanted word which can save the soul. (1:21). James is clearly emphasizing that the word is instrumental in bringing us to God and keeping us close to God. The word of God, when deeply planted in our lives and allowed to flourish without hindrance to its growth from self-seeking or ill will, is able to save the soul.[31] The word is in us because God has put it there; it is implanted. "James speaks here of a kind of 'synergy'—a working partnership—between God and humans. This partnership will characterize James's understanding of salvation throughout the letter."[32]

VERSES 22–25

But prove yourselves doers of the word, and not merely hearers who delude themselves.
For if anyone is a hearer of the word and not a doer, he is like a man who looks at his natural face in a mirror;
for once he has looked at himself and gone away, he has immediately forgotten what kind of person he was.
But one who looks intently at the perfect law, the law of liberty, and abides by it, not having become a forgetful hearer but an effectual doer, this man will be blessed in what he does.

James continues to warn against sentimental, ritualistic, and unpractical religion. He calls his readers to be the "doers of the word." The "word" refers to 1:18 and 1:21. For James, to be a faithful hearer is to be a faithful doer. James does not allow a dichotomy between hearing and doing (obedience). This section, along with verses 26–27, is extremely important to the book. Our innermost belief becomes obvious in what we do. It is not enough just to say we believe the gospel. It must make a difference in our lives.[33] To hear is a necessary part of the Christian life. However, hearing, in today's

---

31. Mitton, *Epistle of James*, 65.
32. Walters, *James*, 62–63.
33. Serrão, *James*, 73.

culture, is mainly a mental activity; hearing just means that our ears pick up sounds. But in Hebrew, the word *shema* (עָמַשׁ) describes hearing and also its effects—taking heed, being obedient, doing what is asked. Any parent who yells at their children, "Were you listening?" or "Did you hear me?" when they ignore a command to pick up their rooms understands that listening should result in action. In fact, almost every place we see the word, it means to hear, listen, and obey. It is interesting to note that the word obedience is translated as "*igboran*" by the Yoruba. Literally it means "to hear words." As such a disobedient person is known as "*alaigboran*," literally, one who does not hear. Therefore, for the Yoruba, to hear truly is to obey what is heard. It goes further than that. For the Yoruba, to hear also means to understand. As such, it may be said that one does not hear if one's ear picks up another language but does not understand its meaning. So it could be said that on the one hand, one is hearing what is being said in another language, and on the other hand, one does not understand. In Paul's words, it will be like trumpet making uncertain sounds or a noisy gong (1 Cor 14:6, 13:2). The implication of the foregoing for James is very clear. Mere picking up sounds of God's word is not enough. Rather, one must also seek to understand what it truly means and also to obey it.

James compares those who hear the word and do not obey it to people who look into the mirror and forget what they look like. By way of contrast, those who look into the perfect law—the gospel of freedom in Christ—are not hearers who forget but doers who act.[34] Peter Davids succinctly sums up the import of metaphor of the mirror. He writes:

> The point is that the impression is only momentary: the look in the mirror while combing one's hair may be temporarily absorbing, but it normally bears no practical results when one engages in the business of the day. It is useless. The momentariness and lack of real effect is the point of the parable, not a comparison with a different type of mirror or a different way of seeing.[35]

In verse 25, James uses a stronger verb for seeing here than in verse 24. The word *parakypsas* literally means "to stoop down," "to bend over" in order to have a closer look (cf. John 20:5, 11). It is used in 1 Pet 1:12 of angels who longed to be able to look more deeply into the wonder of the salvation wrought by Christ on the cross. It is a word which suggests that very close attention is being given to what is being examined. James recommends the example of "the one who looks closely into the perfect law." The one who looks intently into something takes the time really to contemplate what is

---

34. Vanhoozer, *Hearers and Doers*, 204.

35. David, *Commentary on James*, 98.

there—even the things that are beneath the surface. Close self-examination calls for change.

Here *law* (*nomos*) occurs for the first time in James. He uses it in an absolute sense (2:9, 10, 11; 4:11) and describes it in 2:8 as "the royal law." Here it is "the perfect law, the law of freedom." James calls it *perfect* (*teleion*), like the gifts God gives (1:17; see 1:4). For James the law is more than prohibitions but includes moral example. The law acts as a mirror through which a believer is to see how he or she is to act. James adds another verb after this stronger word for seeing. Those who "remain" with the perfect law contemplate its personal implications for their lives. They not only hear the Law but also spend time studying the Law to understand its deep meaning and practical application. This is the law that gives freedom.

In contrast to the forgetful person (vv. 23–24) stands the doer. James adds: "this one will be blessed in his doing." Such people see, hear, contemplate how they will respond, and then they act. And God blesses them for this obedience. Those who have reflected on divine instruction put into practice what they learn.

VERSES 26–27

If anyone thinks himself to be religious, and yet does not bridle his tongue but deceives his own heart, this man's religion is worthless.
Pure and undefiled religion in the sight of our God and Father is this: to visit orphans and widows in their distress, and to keep oneself unstained by the world.

James's admonition in verses 26–27 speaks to the African reader in a special way. African people are known for their religiosity. For many Africans, religion is not separate from the other aspects of one's culture, society, or environment. It is a way of life, and it can never be separated from the public sphere. Religion informs everything in traditional African society, including political art, marriage, health, diet, dress, economics, and death. But the stories of corruption, financial malpractices, and other evil practices on the African continent today betrays her claim to true spirituality. The real outward marks of a religious person are honesty and personal integrity in all areas of life. In these verses James not only continues to underscore the importance of his readers being doers of the word, he also provides and underscores two concrete examples of how it can be done. First, he focuses on the use of the tongue, a subject that he will explore further in chapter 3. James isolates a sin which people are likely to ignore or make light of—the sin of the "unbridled tongue." He has already made reference to the danger in 1:19. Sharp, hurtful words, and also words, however gently spoken, which hint at evil or bad motives are to be eschewed. Second, he focuses on the care of orphans and widows—two vulnerable and often neglected groups in many societies, particularly Africa. It is not, of course, that James intends that loving care should be limited to them. Rather they are mentioned to represent all those who suffer in distress. In those days they were more likely and liable to the miseries of wants and insecurity—children too young to fend for themselves and left fatherless, and women, perhaps with the responsibility of providing for the family. These groups often faced want, and they were always in danger of exploitation and ill treatment.

In mentioning the case of these two groups, James takes his cue from the Old Testament. The *"fatherless"* are first mentioned in Exod 22:21-24, where God warns: "You shall not abuse any widow or orphan. If you do abuse them, when they cry out to me, I will surely heed their cry; my wrath will burn, and I will kill you with the sword, and your wives shall become widows and your children orphans." Here God himself assumes the role of protector of the defenseless orphans and widows. God shows his extraordinary concern for the widows and orphans by issuing this command, and the failure to obey will result in judgment. God himself is described as "a father of the fatherless and a judge for the widows" (Ps 68:5). God expects his people to share the same concern and act accordingly. Whoever tries to distort justice due the vulnerable is pronounced cursed (Deut 27:19). The prophet Isaiah also speaks about the situation of orphans and the dire consequences of mistreating them. He exhorts the people of Israel to "seek justice, reprove the ruthless, defend the orphan, plead for the widow" (Isa 1:17). However, the corruption of the people and their leaders has led them to abandon the vulnerable in society, and for that, they are brought to account: "Your princes are rebels and companions are thieves. Everyone loves a bribe and runs after gifts. They do not defend the orphan, and the widow's cause does not come before them" (Isa 1:23). As a consequence of such callousness and neglect, God told the people of Israel in no uncertain terms: "I will pour out my wrath on my enemies. . . I will turn my hand against you . . . rebels and sinners shall be destroyed together" (Isa 1:24-31). James uses orphan imagery to express the defenselessness of people who are not necessarily orphans but who can relate to the orphan experience because they have been marginalized or displaced. When the people of Israel lament the destruction of Jerusalem by the Babylonians, they liken themselves to orphans: "We have become orphans, fatherless; our mothers are like widows" (Lam 5:3). In their grief, they describe their own orphan status as one in which their inheritance has been given to strangers, their homes have been given to aliens, they must pay for water to drink, and they have no rest. This description is all too similar to present-day experiences of African orphans. Once again, people who are in positions of vulnerability and defenseless-ness appeal to God for help. Jas 1:26–27 provides the final biblical mandate concerning orphans.

The mandate to care for orphans and widows is rightly placed within a larger exhortation to be *doers* and not just *hearers* of God's word. James clearly advocates social engagement as part of Christian purity. Several denominations and churches in Africa continue to wrestle with the rela-tionship between evangelization and social action. What is primary? For James, such question leads to a false choice. Kamell rightly sums up Karl Barth's thoughts that the dichotomy of individual holiness and social activ-ism amounts to a theological failure to understand the unity of justification and sanctification.[36] Such dichotomy results in two errors. While on the one hand it produces the idea of a God who works in isolation leading to an indolent quietism and, on the other hand, the neglect of the relationship between both leads to the notion of a favored person who works in isola-tion, and therefore to an illusory activism.[37] James does not envisage a "do-nothing" faith. It is a call to social action and a challenge to the church to do away with the false dichotomy of evangelism and social action.

It is sad to note that, although growth of the church in the Global South has been a subject of interest among missiologists, an important area that continues to be neglected is the care for orphans and widows. In its report titled *Africa's Orphaned Generation* compiled in 2003, the United Nations International Children's Fund estimated that there were about 11 million orphans in sub-Saharan Africa.[38] It also projected an increase in number in the coming years. James is convinced that for anyone to attain perfection, he or she must look intently into the perfect law of liberty, abide in it, and act upon it (v. 25). We need to be constantly reminded of our identity as follow-ers of Christ, people whose lives have now been transformed by the grace of God. The mirror does just that. For James, it is essential to practice the word and not just hear it. Hearing without doing is of no value and is evidence of truncated living. James is more specific, linking hearing and doing to the use of the tongue as well as the care for orphans and widows. In the same manner as in the Old Testament, it is nearly impossible to discuss orphan status without discussing widow status in African societies. The two are

36. Kamell, "James 1:27," 16.

37. Barth, *Church Dogmatics*, 505, as cited by Kamell, "James 1:27."

38. Unicef. https://healtheducationresources.unesco.org/library/documents/africas-orphaned-generations.

inextricably bound, as evidenced by the numerous biblical passages linking them in the former, and the lived experience of African communities in the latter. African churches need to be more involved in the care for the poor. One wonders if the money expended on private jets by many prominent African leaders could not have been put to a better use by taking care of the widow and the orphan.

CHAPTER 2

James 2:1—26

MOST SCHOLARS AND COMMENTATORS agree that James 2 comprises two sections, namely verses 1–13 and 14–26. The former deals with the sin of partiality, and the latter addresses the issue of the relationship between faith and works. James also prompts his readers to note that faith without action is the equivalent of dead faith. James stresses the need for Christians to show no favoritism on account of wealth, birth, rank, or apparel. He illustrated a case in which two people come into a congregation; one is classily dressed and the other clad in a despicable manner. He said that the people in the community should not show special favor to the latter while assigning the former a modest place.

James highlighted the reasons to avoid partiality, including that God has chosen the poor because the rich oppressed them and were often found among revilers. He called upon believers to love their neighbors since the love of the man was not reserved for only those in beautiful or fanciful clothing.

James does not countenance a dichotomy between belief and behavior, faith and works. For James, believing the word requires obedience. James explained this point by pointing out the example of Abraham, who was justified by the act of sacrificing his only son, Isaac, at the altar. Abraham, as a result of his action, was declared to be righteous in the eyes of the Lord. He combined his faith with action, just as God instructs believers to do. James also cited the example of Rahab who by faith hid the spies. Christian communities should be caring and sharing communities.

VERSES 1-13

My brethren (brothers and sisters[1]), do not hold your faith in our glorious Lord Jesus Christ with an attitude of personal favoritism.

For if a man comes into your assembly with a gold ring and dressed in fine clothes, and there also comes in a poor man in dirty clothes,

and you pay special attention to the one who is wearing the fine clothes, and say, "You sit here in a good place," and you say to the poor man, "You stand over there, or sit down by my footstool,"have you not made distinctions among yourselves, and become judges with evil motives?

Listen, my beloved brethren: did not God choose the poor of this world to be rich in faith and heirs of the kingdom which He promised to those who love Him?

But you have dishonored the poor man. Is it not the rich who oppress you and personally drag you into court?

Do they not blaspheme the fair name by which you have been called?

If, however, you are fulfilling the royal law according to the Scripture, "YOU SHALL LOVE YOUR NEIGHBOR AS YOURSELF," you are doing well.

But if you show partiality, you are committing sin and are convicted by the law as transgressors.

For whoever keeps the whole law and yet stumbles in one point, he has become guilty of all.

For He who said, "DO NOT COMMIT ADULTERY," also said, "DO NOT COMMIT MURDER." Now if you do not commit adultery, but do commit murder, you have become a transgressor of the law.

So speak and so act as those who are to be judged by the law of liberty.

For judgment will be merciless to one who has shown no mercy; mercy triumphs over judgment.

James 2:1-13 is a single sustained argument against the sin of prejudice—an evil that not only continues to manifest itself in various ways in both the church and society. Verse 1 states the thesis: those who have faith in Jesus Christ should be impartial. Verses 2-4 offer a vivid illustration of the violation of this principle. The following three verses maintain the illogicality of such partiality. Verses 8-9 ground the injunction against partiality and discrimination in the biblical principle of love. Verses 10-11 seek to establish that such prejudice makes one a lawbreaker. The final verses call the reader back to the "royal law" of love and mercy, which renders all discrimination between persons as heinous a violation of the law as adultery and murder.

---

1. Addition mine.

To explain the meaning of James 2:1–13, one must situate it in the context of James's warning in 1:21–27. James urges the readers to be doers of the word and not hearers alone in that section. Doing the word is likened to looking at the mirror, which allows the readers to see the gap or discrepancies between their belief and behavior and consequently transform their actions. The first and concrete example that James urges his hearers/readers to pay attention to as they look at the mirror and recognize themselves is the problem of partiality.

Verse 1 is the thesis statement of 2:1–13. It is best understood as an imperative: "Brothers and Sisters, show no partiality." The word translated as "partiality" (Greek, *prosōpolēpsías*) is rare in the New Testament (see also Rom 2:11, Eph 6:9, Col 3:25). It derives from the Hebrew idiom, *panim nasa*, which means "to lift the face on a person." It is an appropriate metaphor for prejudice or favoritism, which implies looking up to one person to look down on another. It is translated by the Yoruba as "*ojusaaju*" which means "face before another face," which is treating people based on considerations other than who they are as persons. The Zulu translation of the word well captures the evil of partiality as '*iphela emasini kule ndaba*,' a phrase that means "there is a roach in this matter" and refers to the removing a cockroach from sour milk. Sour milk is one of the staple foods in South Africa. So when a roach falls into it, the tendency is to take it out and throw it away because it is not edible or valuable to you. In connection to James 2:1, it means that favoritism towards the rich and powerful within the community of faith is as out of place as a roach in the milk. Everybody should be treated the same way in spite of his or her social standing or status.

A Swahili proverb, "*Mnyonge hana haki*," which means "a weak person has no right," underscores the problem of partiality and favoritism in Kenya. So what James is admonishing resonates well with African realities.

James speaks of the incompatibility of partiality with "the faith of our Lord Jesus Christ." A Kikuyu proverb that "there is not the son of the front and the son of the back" well explains James's abhorrence of partiality of favoritism. The proverb is used to rebuke someone who is showing favoritism, where the son in front is the person being favored and the son at the back is starving. It is an aberration for one to profess faith in Christ and at the same time remain prejudiced. To do so fails to follow the example of the Lord when it comes to treating all people with respect, regardless of social status and gender. When the religious leaders of Jesus's day saw him invite Zacchaeus, a tax collector regarded by the society as a traitor and one of the worst sinners, to become one of his followers, they were unhappy and indignant. He treated a woman caught in adultery with dignity (John 8:1–7), refusing to treat women as mere tools or properties to be used, unlike in many patriarchal African societies.

The episode at the beginning of the sixth chapter of Acts resonates with the kind of situation addressed by James. What this incident makes clear is that, even very near its beginning, the early church was beset by partiality and favoritism as it strove to provide for the needs of the Christ-followers. Some were neglected due to their origin: Greek-speaking Jews from outside Judea were being ignored during food distribution. James's warning strikes at the heart of one of the problems in Africa both in society and the church—the issue of ethnocentricity. James warns us against racial or ethnic prejudice. The world has created a sociological pyramid where people boast about their racial superiority and ethnological conceits. The African reader, in particular, retain no doubt concerning the meaning of James 2 with regards to prejudice. In contemporary Africa, partiality based on ethnic identity and tribe of origin is rampant among religious leaders. Nigeria is a case in point. It is not difficult to see that many church leaders are surrounded by others from the same tribe. As defined by Nothwehr, "Tribalism is the attitude and practice of harboring such a strong feeling of loyalty or bonds to one's tribe that one excludes or even demonizes those 'others' who do not belong to that group."[2] Tribalism thus prompts one to have a positive attitude towards those connected to them through kinship, family, and clan. It de facto (directly or indirectly) alienates one from people of other tribes not related to them by blood, kinship, family, or clan.[3] For example, in the Great Lakes region in Kenya, the shape of one's nose was the basis of favoritism.

Sometimes, congregations start based primarily along ethnic and tribal lines. Nkansah-Obrempong traces the heightening of ethnic consciousness in Africa to colonization and the evangelization of Africa during the colonial period. He notes that "the missionaries evangelized particular ethnic groups, resulting in creating ethnic churches and denominations that are predominantly composed of a particular ethnic group."[4] Unfortunately, as he further states, "For all purposes, the church and political leadership have used ethnicity negatively in the context of Africa's socio-economic and political sphere."[5] Someone said that even if Jesus were to run for political office in Kenya he cannot be elected by Christians because he does not come from any of the forty-five tribes of Kenya.

2. Nothwehr, *That They May Be One*, 5.
3. Nwaigbo, "Tribalism Versus Evangelization," 137.
4. Nkansah-Obrempong, *Foundations*, 252.
5. Nkansah-Obrempong, *Foundations*, 252.

Speaking on the problem of apartheid in South Africa, Crocombe opined that the majority of the members of Seventh-day Adventist Church in South Africa were not just complicit but also were wholehearted participants in the South African government's policy of apartheid. He notes that "such participation and support came easily, as there was already a great deal of racial separation and discrimination present in the Seventh-day Adventist church"[6] Perhaps there is no worse demonstration of the adverse effects of ethnocentricity in the church as the Rwandan genocide of 1994 when church members were involved politically and sided with their tribal relatives at the expense of the biblical principle of "oneness in Christ"— a principle that transcends gender, ethnic, or racial barriers. The church, in particular, must avoid the superficial distinction of people. Musopole is certainly right when he observes:

> I have come to believe that the validity of any theological system depends not only on its logical or theological coherence but even more on the way that truth is embodied by those who claim it. It is false theology to claim that all people are made in the image of God and then live to oppress a whole people just because they were created black or women because they did not discover gun powder in time to conquer and dominate. Divorcing doctrine from ethics and subjugating both to racial superiority distorted not only the doctrine of God but of humanity as well.[7]

Looking back at the history of the church, particularly in the fourth century, one could see how elitism crept into the church's life as the "professional clergy" took over the church's entire ministry.[8] The poor and the laity were disenfranchised, while the rich and famous who could afford to pay for penance were favored. Over the past century and recent decades, many churches in Africa that started with missions to the poor folks have all but abandoned their original founding mission statements and practice and have, instead, shifted their focus to the middle and upper classes. Many churches in Africa have gravitated towards the rich and the famous, enhancing the prosperity message of some of their preachers.

Verses 2–4 present a graphic illustration of partiality and prejudice. This example probably does not depict an actual incident but is a stark portrayal in typical diatribe style, drawing its contrasts as vividly as possible. Looking at this passage through the African mirror, one immediately recognizes the African "Big Man" syndrome, which usually refers to the ethos

6. Crocombe, "Seventh-day Adventist Church in Southern Africa."

7. Musopole, *Being Human in Africa*, 175.

8. See especially Miller, *Internal History*, ch. 8.

of leaders in African society that has found its way into the church. The syndrome describes wealthy and influential leaders within the African context. To "carry the briefcase" or the "Bible" in the case of pastors and spiritual leaders is an expression of loyalty and respect. Such leaders surround themselves with an entourage of people, many of them serving as personal bodyguards. It is usual for the "big man/woman" to come to public meetings late and leave earlier than the rest, thereby showing their importance.

A rich person enters the Christian assembly. The gold ring and gorgeous attire mark the rich person's high social rank and wealth. These are in stark contrast to the shabby clothes of a poor person who also enters the assembly. In some churches in Nigeria, there are designated seats for certain persons that must not be occupied by someone else, whether those individuals are in attendance or not. The "owners" of such seats are benefactors who donate large sums of money to the congregation. The rich person is warmly welcome and implored to come and take their seat while the poor person is either left standing, unattended to, or beckoned to sit on the floor at the feet of the rich. James applies the obvious lesson with a question: "When you do such things, do not you make discriminating judgments among yourselves and thus become judges who render corrupt decisions?" Showing favoritism is nothing less than an insult to those who are equally created in the image of God. God does not look at outward appearance in distributing his blessings. Both the poor and rich enjoy the blessing of rain in the same manner that the sun shines upon us regardless of color or class; God's Son offered his lifeblood as a ransom equally for poor and rich. We must not judge people by what they have but what they are. We have no right to be prejudiced against a person merely because he or she is not a person of means. It is sad that, as Sewakpo notes, "in contemporary Nigeria, the practice of royal, political and religious godfathers has become the order of the day." He says that it is practiced with all pleasure and impunity.[9] People are appointed to positions not necessarily on the basis of their qualifications but on their connections with the powers that be. Tinubu, a former governor of Lagos State who assisted his protégé in succeeding him, was reported to have told his protégé in blunt words that, "if there is no partiality, you won't be governor yourself."[10] The issue of partiality and favoritism regarding appointments to political office and securing gainful employment has come with a high price in Nigeria. Unfortunately, the youth have often resorted to violence, rebellion, militancy, and wanton destruction of property. The voice of James needs to be heard, and very clearly at that.

9. Sewakpo, "Relevance of James," 107–8.
10. Premium Times, "Tinubu, Fashola clash at birthday colloquium," para. 3.

For James, when we show favoritism, we become like evil judges who manipulate justice in favor of the rich and rob the poor of justice and fairness against an oppressor. This frequently occurs because those judges have been bribed. When the church, as the people of God, discriminates based on social status, education, or gender, it neglects those who are spiritually minded and accords special privileges to the few who may not even be qualified. It is an all-too-common experience in Africa that nominating committees often choose men and women more for their bank balances than for their abilities, characters, and spirits. In summary, it is wrong to show favoritism in the household of God. Christians must share the love of Christ with all—and honor their fellow heirs in Christ—regardless of differences in gender, skin color, social status, and even age. It goes against the teachings of our Lord, and it will receive severe judgment on the day of his visitation. Where such an attitude prevails in society, the church must turn the tide rather than go with the flow.

James asserts that his hearers' experience at the hands of the rich reveals the absurdity of their preferential treatment of the rich (2:5–7). In the first place, God chose not the rich but those who were poor by the world's standards as heirs of the kingdom (v. 5). James's point is not to advocate a preferential option for the poor but to accentuate his point that acceptance with God is not predicated upon one's material wealth. Indeed, the poor seem to demonstrate a greater acceptance of God, given the social composition of the church. It is observable that it is from the poor, especially in the majority world, that people are more readily won into the Christian faith. On the contrary, the rich, who often do not see the need for God, often express bitter hostility against the Christians.

James's statement about the poor may refer subtly to the social composition of the church. There is an echo of Paul's words in 1 Cor 1:27. God has chosen what was "foolish in the world to shame the wise, and what was weak in the world to shame the strong." As in Corinth, there were perhaps some Christians of means in these communities, but the majority were poor. Although poor as far as material wealth is concerned, they are considered wealthy by God's standards—rich concerning their faith and consequently as heirs of God's kingdom. When God chooses the poor, it is to make them rich, but not as the world counts riches. A possible reflection of Jesus's beatitude is seen here: "Blessed are the poor in spirit, for theirs is the kingdom of heaven" (Matt 5:3). The background to this thought is probably the solid Jewish tradition of the "pious poor," that often those richest in their faith and devotion to God are those poorest in earthly goods. Partiality is nothing but a form of dehumanization and the degradation of human dignity.

By making distinctions based on external factors, the church dishonors the poor and, in doing so, aligns itself with God's enemies.

The conclusion could not be more explicit for James: God shows no reverence to the rich. He has chosen primarily you poor. And your treatment at the hands of the rich should lead you to the same conclusion. Do they repay your partiality to them? No, instead, "they exploit you" (v. 6). James may well have in mind the sort of situation reflected in 5:4-6, where the rich are depicted as holding back by fraud the just wages of their defenseless employees. Likewise, "they drag you into court." These verses probably reflect a situation of social litigation involving wages, debts, and rents where the influential wealthy generally had the upper hand. To top it all, it is the rich who "blaspheme the name (of Christ) by which you are called" (v. 7). It is difficult to determine the specific content of the blasphemy James has in mind. However, it seems that the hostility of the rich is not limited to their bad treatment and hurtful actions against the poor. They are also contemptuous of the honored name of the Lord. He may be referring to wealthy Christians who resort to law courts and so blaspheme the church by exposing its dirty linen in public, as Paul criticized the Corinthians for doing (1 Cor 6:1-6). More likely, it is a general reference to the antagonism experienced when their convictions and preaching brought Christians into conflict with the financial interests of their wealthy neighbors (cf. Acts 16:19-24, 19:23-41). In any event, things are turned around. The rich are honored and the poor dishonored (v. 5). It goes against God's election and their own experience and makes little sense to James.

In verses 8-9, James advances his discussion about partiality by showing that it violates the "royal law."[11] In the process, he quotes Lev 19:18, which falls within one of the most critical passages in the Old Testament that focus on the holiness of the people of God (communal holiness) and is prominently featured in Christian ethics, being showcased also by both Jesus (Matt 22:39 and parallels) and Paul (Rom 13:9, Gal 5:14). This leads to two important points. First is that the holiness of God's people can be described in terms of love. The second is that partiality is wrong because it violates the equality that should characterize the people of God as a community. This is especially clear as one looks at the broader context of Lev 19:18. Verse 15 explicitly condemns partiality: "You shall do no injustice in judgment; you shall not be partial to the poor nor defer to the great, but you are to judge your neighbor fairly."

---

11. John Wesley calls it "the supreme law of the great King which is love; and to every man, poor as well as rich, ye do well" (Lev 19). See Wesley, *Explanatory Notes,* 600.

From an African perspective, partiality violates the *ubuntu* (humanness) spirit that defines Africans as a people. Ubuntu is an African Zulu word that best describes the spirit and philosophical foundation for African living. A vision of human interrelatedness is embedded in the dictum *umuntu ungumuntu ngabantu*, "a person is a person through others." As Clarke notes, "the essence of this aphorism is basic respect and compassion for others."[12] In many African societies the "royal fathers" (kings) are considered as "second to the gods. " As such, any infraction of the king's command is considered a sin and is punishable. The designation of the law as royal shows its inviolability. This fits well with James 2.

But James is not done: he will not let Christians who show partiality off the hook easily. So, in verse 9, he explicitly calls partiality sin, not a mere behavioral aberration. While feeling or admitting that partiality is less than the Christian ideal, many Christians regard it as "unfortunate" rather than grossly evil. James, however, does not entertain such prevarication. Partiality is an evil thing, a defiance of God's will. James does not make room for a cavalier attitude among those who engage in partiality. They may be inclined to dismiss their sin as a trivial fault. Indeed, they may feel that their obedience to the Law in "more important" matters will compensate for such a minor infraction. James however asserts that those who show partiality are transgressors and are under the condemnation of the law (2:10–13). In the same way that an adulterer cannot be excused just because he did not commit murder, so the one who shows partiality is likewise liable for violating the law—here especially the command to love one's neighbor as oneself. James thus shows the absurdity of claiming that to break only one command is different from breaking the law as a whole.

VERSES 14–17

What use is it, my brethren, if someone says he has faith but he has no works? Can that faith save him?
If a brother or sister is without clothing and in need of daily food, and one of you says to them, "Go in peace, be warmed and be filled," and yet you do not give them what is necessary for their body, what use is that?
Even so faith, if it has no works, is dead, being by itself.

James had previously spoken strongly against "hearing" the word without doing what it commanded (1:22–27). Here in verses 14–17 he addresses

12. Clarke, *Pentecostalism*, 114.

"believing" that does not become reality through "doing." James shows the interconnectedness of faith and works—one cannot exist without the other. An authentic faith is to be demonstrated in what it does, not by inaction, passivity, or lack of concern for others. For James, a relationship with Christ ought to produce works. In other words, followers of Jesus are identifiable by what they do. Christian conduct is of immense concern to James. For him, a confession of faith in God and Christ that does not shape the way Christians treat others is empty and unreal. James's pointed, rhetorical questions in verses 14–15 show the seriousness of his concerns: "What use is it, my brothers and sisters, if someone says he or she has faith but has no works? Can that faith save that person? If a brother or sister is without clothing and in need of daily food, and one of you says to them, 'Go in peace, be warmed and be filled,' and yet you do not give them what is necessary for *their* body, what use is that?" These verses set forth one of a number of litmus tests offered throughout the letter as a means of testing the authenticity of one's faith. James is very concerned with the practical and ethical implications of the believer's profession of faith. As Mitton notes, "a profession of sympathy which is no more than polite talk, and which does not lead to helpful action, when such action is our power, is mere sentimentalism."[13]

The vocabulary of "salvation" that James uses in the text is very striking. There are three implications. First, usually when modern, Western believers speak of salvation, they refer to something "spiritual." Not so for James. In the same way as an African, James here does not make a distinction between the salvation of the soul/spirit and that of the body. As a Yoruba saying goes, "*Eni ebi npa ko gbo iwaasu*" ("a hungry person does not listen or need a sermon"). So, James speaks about saving a brother or sister that is hungry and destitute. In light of the usage of "salvation" language later in 5:16, where James links the prayer of faith to the "saving" of the sick, James can be seen to portray salvation as wholistic, involving the whole human person—in the same manner as an African. This is opposed to the disembodied concept of salvation that is often espoused in the Western world due to the understanding of personhood either in terms of the dichotomy of body and soul (or spirit) or the trichotomy of body, soul, and spirit. Second, James's use of familial language recommends the nondiscriminatory attitude that ought to characterize the relationship among believers as members of God's household. Third, James refuses to lend credence to the false and forced choice between evangelism and social action, an argument that has been perpetuated since the 1970s. An authentic faith is demonstrated in action. Profession without performance is pointless. Hence James asks, "What good

13. Mitton, *Epistle of James*, 99.

is it?" and "Can faith save you?"[14] It is action that is the outward manifestation of salvation. James's argument is that faith alone does not reveal one's relationship with Jesus Christ. Works are a living part of a living faith.[15] One who professes to have faith must show it in his or her daily living.

Faith alone will not save just as works alone will not save. Faith and works must be connected for the sake of both inward reality and outward testimony. James fills in the gap between the wealthy and poor, pulling the two together to represent one's faith through works. A person shows selflessness when thinking less of "self" than others. Jesus's purpose was to serve others. James magnifies works since these are the necessary expression of genuine faith. When believers see a hurting individual among them and help that person, they are portraying the actions of Christ. This is an outward manifestation of one's faith and salvation.[16] Christians will be known by their works.

James demands helping the oppressed (2:16). The example he provides seeks to show how "faith alone" is not enough. Merely telling another in despair to "go in peace" or "I am praying for you" leaves faith without fruit when God is calling us to demonstrate the genuineness of our faith through our works. To these poor, unhappy people, short of an adequate supply of material needs such as sufficient food and clothes, the only consolation offered is a cheerful greeting, with cordial good wishes for future comfort but no practical help at all. One of you says, "Go in peace, be warmed, and be filled." Thus, the kind words are used to mask or disguise the harshness of the actual treatment. To the speaker, those words seem to exempt them from the need for any practical kindness. So, no action is taken to supply warm clothes or an assured food supply. There is a story of a man who walked in to see his friend after the latter had just finished praying over the family meal that God would bless and provide for those who were in need. The neighbor came in to request some monetary assistance to help provide food for his family because they had nothing to eat that night. The friend responded that someone had already asked him for a loan, and he just sold his farm products and planned to give the money to the person seeking the loan. The neighbor went out disappointed and dejected. But one of the man's children asked whether the prayer for the poor a few minutes earlier was not supposed to be answered by his father giving the man some of the

---

14. McKnight, *Letter of James*, 224.

15. McKnight, *Letter of James*, 224.

16. Batten, "Jesus Tradition," 381–90.

food items in the house. He was convicted and had to call his neighbor and gave him the needed help to take care of his family.[17]

In such situations as in the previous story, action is required. God uses people to meet the needs of the hurting. Ziglar says, "The community of faith is to be judged based on its actions and not its words."[18] Telling someone to go in peace does not help their physical problem. When this occurs, faith is heard but not seen. The words spoken express belief, but this "faith" effects no change. The oppressed is still dealing with cold and hunger. James's example in 2:16–17 puts 2:1–7 into perspective. There is no partiality or favoritism to be shown to people. Jesus did not pick and choose who he died for. His love was for everyone. Jesus certainly did not pick whom he would serve. Jesus came to serve everyone. Chester and Martin explain that giving to the poor is an attribute of the wise.[19] The poverty written about is not specifically and only in the church. Poverty is seen in everyday life. James instructs the church that faithful living respects the poor.

Interestingly, James uses a different word for the poor. In addition to the term used for the "beggarly poor" (*ptochos,* four times, 2:2–6), his vocabulary includes "the humble poor" (*tapeinos,* 1:9; cf. 4:6, 10), "the workers," "the harvesters," and "the righteous" (5:4, 6). The beggarly poor are depicted as wearing shabby clothes (2:2, something commonly seen in major cities in Africa) or being naked and without daily food (2:15–16). The weak, marginalized, and needy also included women. As Tamez points out, poverty inflicted a double oppression on women,[20] first because of their social status and second because of their poverty. The social status plus James's concern for women in James 2:15 (where James specifically includes "a sister" alongside "a brother" in need) showed his pastoral heart and regard for all people. James's specific mention of "a sister" is probably an indication that there were a significant number of poor of both genders. Women also need to be cared for without partiality. Hoppe elaborates that the poor spoken about in James 2:14–17, "are objects of charity,"[21] people who depended on charity to survive. In this regard, is important to note that James does not attribute the community's poverty to their own making. It was not due to laziness, vices, or generic inferiority. James poses the question to give an illustration to the listeners so that they will put their faith into action. McKnight refers

17. Ishola, *Putting Faith to Work,* 52.
18. Ziglar, "Profit or People First?," 455.
19. Chester and Martin, *Theology of the Letters of James, Peter, and Jude,* 34.
20. Tamez, *Scandalous Message of James,* 20.
21. Hoppe, *There Shall Be No Poor Among You,* 161.

to James 2:14–17 as an example of interrogation.[22] Interrogation is a rhetorical device used to get a person to think about what the speaker is portraying and about the truths that emerge from particular situations. James wants the listeners to derive new and purer motives from their Christian belief.

The verses that follow bring questions in response to the interrogation. Still, James's underlying question is "what good is faith?" (2:14). James brings his point across with another example for the listener to ponder. Maynard-Reid is correct in his observation that "James reveals that one's social involvement in the present is as important as one's religious practices and that personal religion is meaningless without social commitment."[23] This is the foundational undergirding James's statement, "faith by itself, if it has no works, is dead" (2:17).

VERSES 18–19

But someone may well say, "You have faith, and I have works; show me your faith without the works, and I will show you my faith by my works."
You believe that God is one. You do well; the demons also believe, and shudder.

> I'd rather see a sermon than hear one any day;
> I'd rather one should walk with me than merely tell the way;
> The eye's a better pupil and more willing than the ear,
> Fine counsel is confusing, but example's always clear,
> And the best of all the preachers are the men who live their creeds,
> For to see good put into action is what everybody needs.
>
> I soon can learn to do it if you'll let me see it done;
> I can watch your hands in action but your tongue too fast may run.
> And the lecture you deliver may be very wise and true,
> But I'd rather get my lessons by observing what you do;
> For I might misunderstand you and the high advice you give,
> But there is no misunderstanding how you act and how you live.[24]

James's argument about the interrelatedness of faith and works that he just argued continues in the form of a diatribe in verse 18. He anticipates an imaginary interlocutor who might have questions about his argument concerning the interconnectedness of faith and works thus far. Some might say

22. McKnight, *Letter of James.* 224.

23. Maynard-Reid, *Poverty and Wealth*, 98.

24. Guest, *Collected Verse*, 599.

that some have the "gift" of works, and others have the "gift" of faith. There-fore, one with the gift of works should care for the needy while those with faith should exercise the same. James will not allow this kind of thinking. Works will demonstrate genuine faith. The appeal of James is clear and logi-cal. One cannot see faith without works, but one can demonstrate the reality of faith by works. The gross inadequacy of mere intellectual belief in God is clearly demonstrated by the demons, who have a "dead" faith in God. The demons believe in the sense that they acknowledge that God exists. The cor-rectness of their belief does not make them something other than demons; it does not change their practice into that which God would approve or that which would accomplish God's purposes. Gordon Keddie writes:

> They actually have a more informed 'faith' than human hypo-crites! Men and women can make their easy professions of faith and live their worldly lives as if there were no God at all. Their casual blasphemies about 'the man upstairs' can roll off their tongues with never the slightest tremble at the consequences of offending a sovereign and holy God! Why is it that demons tremble, while sinners can sail on in blissful unconcern? The answer is that the demons are not so blind as people. They know their latter end . . . They really fear the wrath to come. But care-less sinners say they believe in God positively, go on in daily life to live as if he did not exist and yet can dream that they are safe in the everlasting arms![25]

Christians in the Western world do not find it easy to think in terms of "demons" but their reality is assumed in the New Testament, whose authors took it for granted that there is a vast world of evil powers ranged against God. Such belief is also prevalent among Africans, hence the multiplicity of many "deliverance ministries." James's statement that "the demons also believe and shudder" is an experiential reality among African Christians.[26] Western critiques of the Pentecostal phenomena and deliverance from de-mons often fail to consider or value the African view of the spirit world. The belief in the existence of other spiritual beings besides God is widespread. In traditional African belief, spirits are ubiquitous: every area of the earth has a spirit of its own and can be inhabited by a spirit.[27] The African universe "is a spiritual universe, one in which supernatural beings play significant

---

25. Keddie, *Practical Christian*, 114.

26. I have been personally involved in ministering to those who are either possessed or oppressed by demons within African and Asian contexts.

27. Idowu, *African Traditional Religion*, 175.

roles in the thought and action of the people."[28] The traditional African lives in a world of unseen intentions where things do not happen by chance. Even when the problems are naturally caused, evil spirits can set in quickly and exploit the situation to the disadvantage of the victim. James suggests identifying the faith of demonic forces with those who merely profess to be believers in Christ without corresponding obedience. In other words, those who claim to belong to God without enacting God's will are in no way different from demons who do likewise. John Wesley's phrase "faith of a devil" is also helpful in understanding James 2:19. He writes:

> I know that I had not faith, unless the faith of a devil, the faith of Judas, that speculative, notional, airy shadow, which lives in the head, not in the heart. But what is this to the living, justifying faith, the faith that cleanses from sin?[29]

Understood in this context, "faith of a devil" simply means a mere assent of the mind to some truth about God and Christ, without an accompanying faith that has the power to shape and order the conduct of one who professes such faith.

VERSES 20–24

But are you willing to recognize, you foolish fellow, that faith without works is useless?
Was not Abraham our father justified by works when he offered up Isaac his son on the altar?
You see that faith was working with his works, and as a result of the works, faith was perfected;and the Scripture was fulfilled which says, "And Abraham believed God, and it was reckoned to him as righteousness," and he was called the friend of God.
You see that a man is justified by works and not by faith alone.

James brings this section to a close by providing an illustration of the character of a living faith in the example of the Old Testament hero, Abraham. He thus cements his argument that a faith unaccompanied by works is a dead faith that cannot save. Before proceeding with his argument, he describes his imaginary interlocutor as "foolish" (v. 20). The word here translated foolish (*kenos*) means empty. It depicts one lacking in a normal good sense. The force of the word is lost in the English translation compared with

28. Gyekye, *Essay in African Philosophical Thought*, 69.
29. Southey, *Life of Wesley*, 214.

the Yoruba translation, "*alaimoye,*" which means "one who has no power of perception," or "thoughtless." It is the height of insult for anyone to be so-called. The imaginary person James addresses fails to recognize the obvious truth because he/she does not have the power of perception.

James moves on to the illustration of Abraham's faith to prove that faith without works is useless. The faith to which James here appeals is displayed by Abraham as recorded in Gen 22. According to Bauckham, that "James's use of the example of Abraham to prove his point is not surprising but virtually predictable, since for Second Temple Judaism Abraham was *par excellence* the exemplar of faith in God."[30] One could see Abraham's faith on three levels. First, as Paul shows, Abraham believed God when facing the seeming impossibility of God's promise to him (Gen 18:10–14, 22:1–24; Rom 4; Gal 3:6). Second, Abraham's faith embraces uncertainty in obeying the command of God when he was told to set out for a land that he did not know. The outcome of his obedience was fraught with danger and insecurity (Heb 11:8).

Third, in what may be termed a climax of Abraham's trials, he showed himself ready to obey God's strange but clear command to sacrifice his only son Isaac (Gen 22). This is the son he loved, considering the remarkable circumstances surrounding his birth and the promise that he would be the vessel for the future of Abraham's offspring. Abraham's obedience was costly—killing the boy without any assurance of another being born, and thus sacrificing the promise itself. This is real faith, one which led him with his eyes wide open into a painful and costly act. His obedience in being willing to offer Isaac demonstrated his unwavering trust in God. In James's estimation, Abraham actually did offer Isaac his son on the altar, even though the angel stopped him from actually killing his son. Yet he had offered Isaac his son in his firm resolution and intentions and would have undoubtedly completed the act had not God stopped him. Abraham was so complete in obedience that he counted Isaac dead as he set him on the altar.

In verses 22–23, James draws the conclusion: Abraham, the quintessential example of true faith, was justified not by faith alone—that is by mere show of words claiming to be faith—but by works which sprang from the reality of his faith. There are many scholarly discussions on what justification means in this context. However, the word *dikaioō* ("to justify") as *idalare* in the Yoruba Bible does not leave the African reader with "multiple choices." It simply means "acquittal."[31] James goes on to say that the faith of Abraham

30. Bauckham, *James*, 122.

31. Unfortunately, this translation does not allow various nuances of the word that is possible in the Greek language. For example, taken by itself, it has no ethical or moral content except when used in its noun form.

was made perfect by his deeds. In other words, by his obedience in willingness to sacrifice Isaac, his faith reached its appointed goal.

In verse 23, James continues his argument by citing Genesis 15:6. Although in the Genesis account Abraham was reckoned righteous by faith (Gen 15:6) long before he offered Isaac (Gen 22), James seems to suggest that it was in the act of his obedience in the latter that the Scripture was fulfilled. It is interesting to know that although the two words "justify" (*dikaioō*) and "righteousness" (*dikaiosyne*) are from the same root, the former tends to be understood as primarily forensic. At the same time, the latter is capable of several meanings depending on usage hence its translation. "*ododo*" in the Yoruba Bible and *ezi omume* in the Igbo language. In Hausa, a righteous person is described as *mutumin kwarai*. In all these instances, righteousness is understood in an ethical/moral sense and, as such, an aspect of holiness. This is close to the meaning of the word "perfect" in verse 22. Batten's comments on the importance of Abraham's example are worth quoting at length. She writes:

> Abraham functions, not only as a proof in the form of an example, but a model of how a human being can be a friend of God. It is through testing and caring for others that the audience can become friends with God, not through buttering up the rich. . . . Abraham does not behave like a patron, demanding honour, but freely provides hospitality to strangers. Abraham is a model for how the community members should treat one another, particularly how those who had more should support the most vulnerable.[32]

VERSES 25-26

In the same way, was not Rahab the harlot also justified by works when she received the messengers and sent them out by another way?
For just as the body without the spirit is dead, so also faith without works is dead.

Still discussing the relationship between faith and works, James continues with the story of Rahab. It is quite notable that James immediately follows the example of a revered Jew with that of a woman whose character remains a matter of scholarly debate.[33] James evokes the faith of Rahab to indicate

---

32. Batten, *Friendship and Benefaction in James*, 142–43.
33. Charles, "Rahab," 206–20.

that one is made right with God not on the basis of some intellectual assent alone that could be characterized as faith, but on actions demonstrating such confidence in God. She had faith before the spies came to her. She told the spies: ". . . the Lord your God, He is God in heaven above and on earth beneath" (Josh 2:11). Rahab and the other inhabitants of Jericho heard about God before the spies ever came and believed that word (Josh 2:9–14). What she did with the spies was, then, a result of the faith that already existed in her heart. James's point is that, like Abraham, Rahab put her faith into action! Both did not just claim to have faith in God and sit idly. Their faith led them to action.[34]

The fact that Rahab is non-Jewish (gentile) and a woman is not lost on the African woman. Musa Dube writes:

> I never felt closer to her than now. I mean Rahab the sex worker of Jericho. I have been (and I am still) in her house. I have thought her thoughts. I have laughed with Rahab's laughter. I have cried with Rahab's tears, until I realized that maybe I will just have to hang my tears to dry. I have walked her walk to the window of her home, which was built in the wall of the great city of Jericho—a city about to be pulled down, destroyed together with its inhabitants, by those with physical might and divine claims. Together with thousands of other inhabitants of the city, they are counting days to the dreadful day of their destruction. The enemy is gathering around to besiege the city. The sin of Jericho, and its inhabitants, is that they are different and, perhaps, less powerful. As Rahab walks to the window, she stops to glance at the bed by the far end—the bed where she made love with the two spies from the enemy camp. She walks on toward the window and begins to hang the red ribbon. It hangs loosely down the wall so that her enemies must see it and save her, when they destroy the city of Jericho and all its inhabitants.[35]

Dube's position on her proffered reasons the for the destruction of the city of Jericho is debatable but her point about Rahab as an example of the marginalized in society is on target. She is, in every sense, a symbol of the oppressed and marginalized in the society. Rahab is the "Other." The African is still the "other" in many respects, with their voices muted. Yet Rahab's story is placed beside that of a man called the friend of God. Although portrayed as the "Other," she stood on the same platform with Abraham, justified in the same way. As with Abraham, her faith was not a theoretical

---

34. Ellsworth, *Opening Up James*, 100.
35. Dube, "Rahab is Hanging Out a Red Ribbon," 177.

opinion but one that caused her to act daringly and effectively in the service of God and his people, and notably, against the interest of her own people. James uses the body and spirit analogy to prove that faith without works is dead. Rahab, in showing her concern for strangers also provides an example on how the community members should treat one another.[36] As one concludes this passage, it is clear that James's emphasis on works is not an attempt to make light of "faith" but to make what constitutes true faith as clear as possible. James intends to warn against the mere lifeless profession of faith that does not affect how one lives, particularly regarding partiality and hospitality.

36. Batten, *Friendship and Benefaction*, 143.

CHAPTER 3

James 3:1–18

JAMES BEGINS CHAPTER 3 with a caution against those who want to be teachers of the word. Regarding the judgment that awaits them, he said that one should be sure that they possess the maturity and the self-control necessary for controlling their tongue. He then provides some illustrations to demonstrate the tongue's power and danger.

James revealed that some sought to become teachers to look wise. But he goes on to write that wisdom and understanding should be shown by the conduct of a person. A living faith shows itself in its control of what we say. So, James puts a particular emphasis on the use/misuse of the tongue.

In 3:1–12, James cautions against becoming teachers, saying they will receive a stricter punishment unless they are mature and possess self-control virtues. He revealed that the power of the tongue is like a bit that controls the horse or a small rudder that directs the ship.

James was adamant about the dangers of the tongue. He said it is like a fire that kindles a big forest, capable of defiling the body and setting fire to the course of nature. He also talked about the difficulty in taming one's tongue, saying that there is nobody who can control their tongue all the time. It is an unruly evil full of poison that can be used for blessings and curses.

The chapter concludes with a brief discussion about godly wisdom. James contends that worldly wisdom is bitter, self-seeking, lying, and boasting. It is demonic and produces confusion. On the contrary, heavenly wisdom, the wisdom that comes from above, is pure, gentle, peaceful, willing to yield, bears good fruits, and is full of mercy. It is without hypocrisy and partiality. Heavenly wisdom produces righteousness and peace (vv. 13–18).

VERSE 1

Let not many of you become teachers, my brethren, knowing that as such we will incur a stricter judgment.

Teaching is a vital ministry in the church. The growth of the church in the majority world, particularly in Africa, in the past decades has been phenomenal. It is a great reason to celebrate the expansion of the kingdom of God. However, the negative side has been the lack of sound teaching and doctrinal errors and practices. Many African pastors start churches without having formal theological education.[1] They simply wake up one morning and profess that they have been driven or inspired by the Holy Spirit to start a church. Teaching is one of the ministry gifts in the New Testament (1 Cor 12:28, Eph 4:11). Teaching in the churches is not supposed to be done just by anyone standing in front of others to teach. The Lord must gift the person through the Holy Spirit.

Teachers can teach the word of God clearly, accurately handle the word of truth, encourage others by sound doctrine, and refute those who oppose it (1 Tim 3:11, 2 Tim 2:15, Titus 1:9). As suggested in chapter 1, one of the nuances of the word *doulos* in the African context is "disciple," and discipleship is a lifelong process. Since the Christian's calling is to "grow up into Him who is the head," teaching is a critical element to growth in the spiritual life. Educational degrees are not awarded in the Christian life. Once a Christian sets foot on the path of discipleship, the journey never ends.

James has a sober warning for those who would become teachers in the church. They must take the responsibility seriously because their accountability is greater, and they shall receive a stricter judgment. It is easy to take the position of teacher lightly in the church without considering its cost in terms of accountability. Here James echoes the words of Jesus in Luke

---

1. My point is not to assert that every pastor or teacher must possess an advanced degree in theological education but to underline the problem of erroneous teachings due to lack of training. Even political leaders, particularly in East Africa, are aware of the problem. Paul Kagame, the president of Rwanda, closed many churches and issued a proclamation that there should be no untrained pastors. The governments of Kenya and Zambia are also moving in that direction. Here are Kagame's words: "I have closed over 6,000 churches and mosques in my country and I am now demanding for a theology degree for every religious leader. Stop playing with people's faith and making it a business. Rwanda is already a blessed country" (https://moguldom.com/370885/remembering-when-rwanda-president-paul-kagame-closed-6000-churches-and-mosques-stop-making-it-a-business). Based on conversations with some Christian leaders, I am aware that some Rwandan Christians are suspicious of the move, believing that there is an ulterior political motive.

12:48. Both Jesus and James remind us that being among the teachers in God's church is more than a matter of having natural or even spiritual gifts; there is an additional dimension of appropriate character and right living. The prophet Malachi's words well capture James's thoughts:

> "Then you will know that I have sent this commandment to you, that My covenant may continue with Levi," says the Lord of hosts. "My covenant with him was *one of* life and peace, and I gave them to him *as an object of* reverence; so he revered Me and stood in awe of My name. True instruction was in his mouth, and unrighteousness was not found on his lips; he walked with Me in peace and uprightness, and he turned many back from iniquity. For the lips of a priest should preserve knowledge, and men should seek instruction from his mouth; for he is the messenger of the Lord of hosts. But as for you, you have turned aside from the way; you have caused many to stumble by the instruction; you have corrupted the covenant of Levi," says the Lord of hosts. (Mal 2:4–8)

In like manner as the Levitical priests, teachers of God's word must realize their solemn responsibility as role models who can either build up life or destroy by what they do and speak. The ministry of the teacher is to edify believers, to turn people away from sin, and never to become a stumbling block. However, it must be noted that although the warning could have primary reference to teachers, the lessons in the following verses apply to all his audience.

VERSES 2–5

For we all stumble in many ways. If anyone does not stumble in what he says, he is a perfect man, able to bridle the whole body as well.
Now if we put the bits into the horses' mouths so that they will obey us, we direct their entire body as well.
Look at the ships also, though they are so great and are driven by strong winds, are still directed by a very small rudder wherever the inclination of the pilot desires.
So also, the tongue is a small part of the body, and yet it boasts of great things. See how great a forest is set aflame by such a small fire!

Verse 2, although not unconnected with James's warning to teachers in verse 1, provides a transition from the responsibility of teachers (2a) and proceeds to deal with Christians in general (2b–5). Hence verses 2b–5 connects with other James passages where he deals with the same subject (1:19, 26; 2:12; 3:6–12; 4:11; 5:9, 12). The evil that comes from words can hardly be exaggerated. Many African countries have experienced phantom military coups at different times. An example of such was in Nigeria in 1997. The ruling government at that time arrested several people who allegedly participated in the coup, but some of them were innocent. Some were sentenced to death though later commuted to years in imprisonment. But for the sudden death of the military head of state, innocent people would have languished in prison for the rest of their lives just because of the wrong use of the tongue!

As though someone would have protested that the tongue, as small as it is, could not exert as much influence over the body that James ascribes to it, James gives three illustrations to make his point. The first is a horse that can be tamed by putting a bit in its mouth. The bit in the horse's mouth is tiny compared with the size of the horse itself, yet by it, the horse can be controlled and directed. James's second illustration is the use of the rudder in controlling the ship. The rudder is insignificantly small compared with the vessel's mass, yet the rudder sets the ship's course in the water. A wrong turn with the rudder can lead to a severe disaster, running the ship into icebergs and breaking it into pieces. The *Titanic* is a good example! Tongues, though small members of our bodies, can either be helpful to steer the affairs of family, denomination, or nation in the right direction or bring them to ruin.

James's third analogy is a little fire spark that could destroy thousands of acres of land. The modern experience of devastating forest fires started by a picnic fire or a lighted cigarette end gives a striking effect to this illustration by James. Such is the effect of the tongue when it is let loose. The tongue can wreak much havoc, whether by false teaching in the church or malicious gossip, nasty innuendo, cutting sarcasm, and witty sallies at the expense of one's colleagues or church leaders, self-display and self-commendation.

VERSES 6-12

And the tongue is a fire, the very world of iniquity; the tongue is set among our members as that which defiles the entire body, and sets on fire the course of our life, and is set on fire by hell.
For every species of beasts and birds, of reptiles and creatures of the sea, is tamed and has been tamed by the human race.
But no one can tame the tongue; it is a restless evil and full of deadly poison.

With it we bless our Lord and Father, and with it we curse men, who have been made in the likeness of God; from the same mouth come both blessing and cursing. My brethren, these things ought not to be this way.
Does a fountain send out from the same opening both fresh and bitter water? Can a fig tree, my brethren, produce olives, or a vine produce figs? Nor can salt water produce fresh.

James emphasizes failure to control the tongue; the amount of space he devotes to the discussion is notable. The tongue is a crucial part of the human body. It is the means of expressing how a person feels about issues bothering him or her. Tongues control the way we relate to others, as we can use our tongues wisely or otherwise (vv. 13–18). Many relationships have been ruined because of the misuse of the tongue. The bitter pain of a word spoken against us can hurt us for a lifetime, long after a broken bone has healed. As an African proverb says, "A cutting word is worse than a bowstring; a cut may heal, but the cut of the tongue does not." Such is the power of the tongue. A particular community in southwestern Nigeria describes and prides itself as people who "kill with words instead of swords."[2] The potency of the tongue and the damage that it can do is well-captured by that cognomen. This is a direct contradiction of an often-quoted children's rhyme which says that "sticks and stones may break my bones, but words can never hurt me." That rhyme is not true; words break more than bones words break hearts.

In verse 4, James uses the illustration of the rudder of a ship. Although the imagery of a ship did not easily resonate with a few members of the study group in Nigeria, they were familiar with trucks and trailers that are turned around with steering wheels. The point is clear. Little things can cause significant problems. One may hear an echo of Ecclesiastes 10:1 that shows the impact of little things such as dead flies or the weightiness of a "little foolishness" and Song 2:15[3] in this passage. Several years ago, the Kainji Dam, the main hydroelectric power plant that supplied electricity to Nigeria, was abruptly shut down. The whole nation was plunged into darkness for several days.[4] An investigation into the incident revealed that a small snake had tripped the circuit breaker. Although James, unlike Paul (cf. Rom 3:13), does not use the imagery of a snake to describe the tongue, the poison that it produces (Jas 3:8) points in the same direction. In the

2. Their pride is actually manifested a musical piece played on the radio singing those words.

3. The writer points to the ruin of the vineyards by "little foxes."

4. See, "Disco Dance in the Dark," https://dailytrust.com/amp/disco-dance-in-the-dark.

history of Nigeria, there have been instances where the misuse of the tongue has caused tribal wars. The Yoruba proverb, *Owe l'esin oro,* "proverbs are the horses of communication," shows the power of words equal to a horse's strength and speed.

In verse 5, James likens the tongue to a small fire that sets ablaze a great forest. Here James echoes Old Testament wisdom (see Prov 15:1, 18:21, 26:20). He realizes that Christians can be dangerous when using their tongue. Family and church members can be very mean in their verbal attacks of each member. This is common among the Yoruba of southwestern Nigeria. They are good at abusing maidservants and their children. Some traders or market-women engage in the name-calling of customers who, though they are Nigerians, come from other tribes.

The dethronement of a paramount traditional ruler in Nigeria in the recent past demonstrates the unintended consequences of the use of the tongue. Writing a recap on the entire saga, a journalist of one of the reputable Nigerian newspapers says:

> In recent times, the pronouncements of the Emir have no doubt been acerbic and critical of the Nigerian government. Sanusi did not take any prisoners! With deviant profundity, he exposed the charade of the Northern government. He talked about the abuse of women, the menace of the almajiris, and the need to abolish it. He lampooned the elite and warned them against the abuse of children, especially, the girl child. He lamented the frightening number of the out-of-school children in the North and linked it to the ever-rising number of Boko Haram adherents, drugs addicts and the reservoir of political thugs, which now defines the demography of the Northern part of the country.[5]

James's third analogy for the description of the destructive power of the tongue is fire. A tiny spark of fire has set thousands of acres of fire ablaze. This illustration is at home with many African farmers who, every summer, due to lack of resources, resort to preparing the ground for cultivation by setting the debris on fire.[6] This, of course, has led to severe disasters. The indiscriminate burning of grass continues to deplete good farming land. Consequently, deserts are encroaching so fast, with dangerous effects on the economies of many African nations. But that is not the end. The smoke from the fires turns into fumes that pollute the environment, defiling the air we breathe. The tongue is as powerful as the fire and the smoke.

---

5. Komolafe, "As Emir Sanusi Becomes History."
6. I saw my father do this year after year.

Many countries on the African continent have faced and continue to face civil wars, some due to reckless or irresponsible write-ups or speeches by politicians. As the Yoruba adage goes, *Oro pele yo obi lapo, oro lile yo ida l'apo*: "A soft word brings kola nut from the pocket, and a harsh word brings sword from the sheath." That is to say that words can either lead to an amicable relationship, inviting one to treat the speaker with respect, or can lead to drawing one's sword from the sheath for possible war. So many lives have been ruined due to careless and irresponsible statements. Sarcastic remarks by teachers and parents have destroyed gifted and talented kids. Many churches have been split due to reckless statements by a few individuals, sometimes leaders within the congregation.

James continues the importance of consistency in Christian living in verses 9–12. He deals with the problem of misuse of the tongue within the congregation. Some can sing and pray fervently in the worship service but can use abusive language, be destructively critical of others, or even curse outside the church. For James, one who sings praises to God should not be found cursing. When Christians, particularly leaders, use abusive language or even curse others outside the church, it raises questions about their spirituality. Eloquent prayers in the church accompanied by sarcastic and destructive criticism of others at home and in the marketplace are sheer hypocrisy. Today, cursing seems to be a "respectable sin," and there is a loss of insensitivity to irreverence within the church and the wider society. In contemporary Africa, especially among, but not limited to Pentecostal churches, some "warfare prayers" where curses are constantly rained down on the heads of real and imagined enemies need to be re-examined. Recently, a Nigerian newspaper reported the story of the response of a prominent pastor in Nigeria to an allegation of some wrongdoing by an aggrieved member. Here are his own words:

> Do you want me to go on national television to be replying to an idiot? No, that's a waste of resources. I'm following the Bible (Proverbs 12), anyone who hates correction is stupid. I will now go and get one-hour television airtime and pay N4 million to be responding to an idiot? Don't allow provocation to turn you into a lunatic yourself. Whoever loves instruction loves knowledge but he who hates correction is stupid. When you get to where nobody can correct you, you are stupid, they should leave you alone," Bakare stated.[7]

Christianity is a way of thinking, feeling, acting, and of course, speaking. In these verses, James appears to forcefully say that no person might

7. Eyokoba, "Bakare Replies."

be rightly called a Christian unless they have given their lips and speech to God. A converted heart exhibits itself in a converted tongue. On the other hand, a loose tongue is probably an indication of looseness everywhere, for a wagging tongue indicates a lack of central control in one's personality. The rhetorical question calls for a reply of "Absolutely not!" Fig trees do not yield olives or vine figs. The point is that the tree species determine the type of fruit produced. The condition of one's heart determines the kind of "fruit" from one's mouth, the good fruit of blessing from a redeemed, regenerate heart but a rotten fruit of cursing from an unregenerate evil heart. How and when we open our mouths matter much. When our words are right, they can be a powerful force for good. But when they are wrong, they work like a deadly poison. Instead of being helpful, they are destructive. Rather than building up our friends, our words can tear them down. An African folktale well illustrates this:

> Once, a chief told one of his servants to bring him the best meat from the market. The servant brought him a tongue. The next day the chief told the servant to bring him the worst meat from the market. The servant brought a tongue again. "What?" the chief said. "When I ask for the best meat, you bring a tongue, and then you bring the same thing for the worst meat." The servant said, "Sometimes a man is very unhappy because of his tongue and sometimes his tongue makes him very happy." "You are right," the chief said. "Let us be masters of our tongue!"

VERSES 13-18

Who among you is wise and understanding? Let him show by his good behavior his deeds in the gentleness of wisdom.

But if you have bitter jealousy and selfish ambition in your heart, do not be arrogant and so lie against the truth.

This wisdom is not that which comes down from above, but is earthly, natural, demonic.

For where jealousy and selfish ambition exist, there is disorder and every evil thing.

But the wisdom from above is first pure, then peaceable, gentle, reasonable, full of mercy and good fruits, unwavering, without hypocrisy.

And the seed whose fruit is righteousness is sown in peace by those who make peace.

Earlier in 2:14–16, James questioned the authenticity of the profession of faith without corresponding actions. Those who profess to have faith must demonstrate it by their works. James insisted on proof of one's profession of belief in Christ—belief must result in behavior, leaving no credibility gap. Something of the same dynamic is in 3:13–18. He starts with a rhetorical question to draw the attention of those who claimed to be "wise and understanding" to the implications of such a claim. James shows what wisdom is by comparing it to different lifestyles.[8] The word *sophos* ("wise") used here carries the idea of "exhibiting sound judgment or good sense." The word used for understanding (*epistēmōn*) could also be translated as "knowledgeable," and it means "knowing thoroughly" or "having expertise."[9]

James is seeking to identify who is truly skilled in the art of righteous living. This question is also for any person who professes to be a follower of Christ. He uses the third person imperative to insist that persons supposedly possessing wisdom and intellect should *demonstrate* this *by means of a morally good lifestyle.* Just as he earlier challenged those who claim they have faith to show it by works, he likewise encourages those who profess to be "wise and have understanding" to show it by the results of a righteous life.[10] True wisdom and understanding are not to be identified with merely intellectual cleverness. Their genuineness is demonstrated by the quality of life that they produce. In other words, both are expressed in the very life of the Christian.[11] There is an echo of Old Testament wisdom literature in this verse (cf. Job 28:28; Prov 1:7, 9:10; Eccl 12:13). It is significant that the characteristics James first listed for godly wisdom are purity and gentleness. As such, "wisdom" clearly refers to living an ethical or moral life. "Far from being entombed in the world of the intellect, true wisdom is firmly attached to performance!"[12] The evidence of possession of wisdom is a holy lifestyle. A claim to wisdom not validated by good behavior is as empty as that of faith without corresponding actions to prove it.

It is important to note that gentleness or meekness is at the top of James's list for good behavior. It is one of the qualities that Jesus pronounced as blessed (Matt 5:5). It is the antithesis of resentment and vengeance. This meaning suits the present context well, noting its contrast to selfish ambition and jealousy. Here meekness is the opposite of arrogance, self-assertion, and self-importance. As James has already explained in chapter 2, a genuinely

8. Hartin, *Spirituality of Perfection*, 72.

9. Serrão, *James*, 127.

10. Wesley, *Explanatory Notes*, 55.

11. Hartin, *James and the "Q" Sayings of Jesus*, 100.

12. Keddie, *Practical Christian*, 140.

righteous or holy person will do deeds, and these deeds are to be done in the "gentleness of wisdom." It is a false claim for a person to believe they have wisdom if not expressed in meekness or gentleness.[13] Deeds done in the "gentleness of wisdom" are deeds done in true humility. James's words ring true to Africans who understand wisdom as the root of ethical behavior and are orientated towards promoting the common good and hospitality. As rightly noted by Ogunyemi, the connection between wisdom and ethical conduct is essential and serves as an internal driver. He writes:

> For . . . Yoruba living in different African countries and some African American and Latin American communities, internal drivers include *Iwa*: virtue, character, good behavior; *Ogbon*: wisdom, cleverness or cunning; *Imo*: knowledge; *Oye*. Understanding. The connection can be seen in wisdom sayings such as '*omo to gbon kii s'iwa hu*' meaning 'a wise child does not misbehave.' Hence, the wise leader displays *iwa*, which is virtue and ethical behavior, and in so doing, shows *imo* (knowledge), *oye* (understanding), and *ogbon* (wisdom), and attains the status of *Omoluwabi* when this is done consistently. The term *Omoluwabi* refers back to the community from which the wise leader springs and whom the wise leader serves. It also brings honor to the person's family.[14]

In verse 14, the first on the list of James's characterization of worldly wisdom is bitter zeal (*zēlon pikron*). Overconfidence in the correctness of one's convictions can quickly evolve into "blind fanaticism."[15] The zealot "sees himself as jealous for the truth, but God and others see the bitterness, rigidity, and personal pride which are far from the truth."[16] Stories of bitter rivalry with devastating consequences abound in Africa. The word used by James, *eritheia*, means self-seeking, strife, contentiousness, extreme selfishness, rivalry, one who seeks only his or her own interests. Aristotle uses the term to refer to the selfish ambition, the narrow partisan zeal of factional, greedy politicians, so this word may also convey the notion of rivalry, party spirit, or factiousness. It is not uncommon for politicians in Nigeria to switch political parties as many times as possible, as long as it serves their advantage and advancement. Sometimes they bolt their party and start a new one. This fits well with the word James uses here. The term suggests the vice of a leader who creates a party for his pride. It has no room

---

13. Sidebottom, *James, Jude, 2 Peter*, 49.

14. Ogunyemi, "Indigenous African Wisdom." Italics all mine.

15. Serrão, *James*, 128.

16. David, *Commentary on James*, 151.

for others, much less genuine humility. That ultimate self-elevation rampant in the world today is the antithesis of what the gentle, humble, selfless, giving, loving, and obedient child of God is called to become in Christ by the power of his Spirit. Although sad to admit, the word best sums up both the spiritual and political realities in a majority of the countries in Africa. It is not an uncommon sight in Nairobi to find as many as eight to ten churches meeting in different rooms at the same time within the same building. Often, such "church planting" is driven by rivalry and jealousy.

The second vice is selfish ambition. In Nigeria, the unspoken rivalry among denominations is about who has the largest congregation and worship auditorium. Sometimes, rivalry among preachers is so intense that leaders do not speak to each other. The same is true elsewhere on the continent. In 2018, I was invited to teach a Bible course in Kigali, Rwanda. The meeting was hosted by one of the two largest Pentecostal churches in the city. I was introduced to the pastor of the other denomination. At first, he sounded very enthusiastic about meeting with me. He sent his assistant to me to arrange for a meeting. However, when he learned that I was holding a class in the other church, he stopped all communication with me.

The irony is that I did not even set my eyes on the pastor of the host church throughout my stay (he delegated everything about my visit). I later found out that the members of the two churches are not supposed to relate to one another. How sad! Yet, these church leaders boast of their success. James says that those claiming to be wise and understanding must not boast (*katakauchasthe*) if they have bitter jealousy and self-interested rivalry. What led to the boastful behavior is not clear. Whatever the reason may be for boasting, it is wrong. For James, those who have jealousy and selfish ambition in their hearts have nothing to boast about. James addresses empty and dangerous boasting again in 4:13–17. To do so is to lie against the truth. The command not to deny or *lie against* the truth refers to living in contradiction to Christian teaching ("the word of truth" in 1:18; see Acts 5:3). As believers, this truth is "planted" in them, so they should "humbly accept" (1:21) or "welcome" it "with meekness" (NRSV). This is truth, not so much as a concept as a manner of life. To abandon the Christian lifestyle is to stray from the truth.

In verse 15, James negatively assesses the supposed "wisdom" of those who have bitter zeal and self-interested rivalry in their hearts: "This wisdom is not coming down from above, but is earthly, sensual, and demonic." The participle rendered "coming down" develops the theme introduced in 1:17, where "every good and perfect gift" is said to be "from above, coming down" (see 3:17). So "considered together with 1:5, it is clear that James regards genuine wisdom as a divine gift, a perception deeply rooted in the world of Torah"[17] (cf. Prov 2:6, Job 28:20–28). But James considers the so-called wisdom of the supposedly "wise and understanding" (Jas 3:13) as definitely not from God. Instead, he depreciates it with three adjectives. The first, "earthly," denotes that which is not heavenly, divine, or eternal. The second adjective, "sensual"(*psychikē*), is related to the root *psychē* ("soul"). It is never used in a positive sense in the New Testament. Jude 19 tells us that people who are *psychikoi* ("sensual") "do not have the Spirit." This is likely James's point here. Earthly wisdom is not a fruit of the Spirit. The third adjective James uses to describe bitter and self-interested (v. 14) "wisdom" is "demonic" (*daimoniōdēs*). This vaunted but false "wisdom" is of the devil ("devilish," NRSV). The mention of "demonic" wisdom evokes the memory of idol worshippers in my hometown who boast of being able not only to tell of the present circumstance but also offer help to those who consult them. However, what they do is ferret information from their hosts. This information is then provided to the priest, who, in turn, tells the client who is left wondering how the priest knew. Unfortunately, some churches use the same tactics. There are many stories of fake miracles being performed.[18] If anyone professes to be wise, but their wisdom leads to disorder, disunity, the suffering of many people, or lack of social peace, the so-called wisdom is from Satan.

In verses 17 and 18, James turns his attention to explaining true wisdom. James immediately follows his rhetorical question with an answer that enunciates the character of any wise person in the church. Such a person will exhibit a good life, expressed in actions performed without ostentation or an iota of self-promotion or showmanship. Wisdom is like a fountain of holiness. It produces godly virtues that need to be cultivated instead of vices that must be avoided. James gives a list of eight virtues that wisdom produces. They are not necessarily in any specific order outside of giving prominence to the first two virtues in the list.[19] James explains that godly wisdom is first pure—free from all the previously mentioned impurities.[20] Purity can also mean something that is "unblemished," "without moral defect," or in other words, it is "holy." Godly wisdom, which is "unblemished" or "without moral defect," is not capable of producing evil.[21] James's concern here is not with ritual but practical holiness, as throughout his epistle.

17. Serrão, *James*, 128.

18. For some examples see these links: https://www.pulse.com.gh/ece-frontpage/false-prophets-pastor-woman-arrested-for-staging-fake-miracle-in-church/znw33wg and https://guardian.ng/news/end-of-road-for-woman-used-by-pastors-to-perform-fake-miracles/.

19. Serrão, *James*, 129.

20. Tasker, *General Epistle of James*, 82.

21. Moo, *Letter of James*, 172.

He describes holiness in terms of the sociological categories of purity and character.

The word "pure" represents the Greek word *hagnos*. Although the original background of *hagnos* in many respects coincides with that of *hagios*,[22] in Paul, it simply has the significance of morally clean, pure, innocent, chaste. Paul uses this word in Phil 4:8 as he encourages the reader to be selective in their choice of thinking. Stability of character demands a disciplined thought life. Among the other things worthy of being entertained in our minds, such as the true, the just, the lovely, the virtuous, stands "the pure." It must be a consciously permitted and voluntarily chosen object of thought that conforms to holiness's norm. The same idea is here in this passage. James is speaking of a "wisdom" set apart in contradistinction to the superficial, manipulative wisdom that permeates society. In sum, a person with godly, pure wisdom is a person of integrity.

The wisdom from above is first "pure," but then it is "peaceful." Peace is in contrast to the disorder that is mentioned in verse 16. The Hebrew word for peace, *shalom*, means "wholeness, prosperity, and soundness."[23] Wisdom in the Old Testament also produced peace (Prov 3:17).[24] As a result of redemption, those in Christ are at peace with God (Rom 5:1), and therefore Christians should be "peaceable" with others as well. Christians who walk in wisdom will do everything they can to live in peace. Peace flows out of a relationship with God. Jesus said, "Blessed are the peacemakers, for they will be called children of God" (Matt 5:9). A peace-loving Christian is not a doormat or someone who makes peace for its own sake. Neither does peace-loving mean avoidance of conflicts. Instead, a peace-loving person does not impose their solutions on those who disagree with them.

The wisdom from above is gentle. Gentleness can mean benevolence, courtesy, or generosity.[25] Gentle people are considerate and good to others, and therefore they are "willing to yield." The word signifies humble patience, a steadfastness to submit to injustice, disgrace, and maltreatment without hatred and malice, trusting in God despite everything that may be happening. A person who possesses this wisdom is nonassertive. Instead, they are sensitive to others' needs and forbearing.

Next, James describes wisdom from above as "full of mercy and good fruits." Here James encourages the teachers from verse 1 and others to be "full of mercy and good fruits." The word fruit (*karpōn*) figuratively

22. Moo, *Letter of James*, 172.

23. Serrão, *James*, 130.

24. Moo, *Letter of James*, 172.

25. McKnight, *Letter of James*, 313.

describes the observable results in a person's life (see, e.g., Matt 7:16, 20; Luke 6:43–44; John 15:5, 8). In Paul's letters, fruit is often used in much the same way as James uses actions, visible results. Paul refers to "the fruit of the Spirit" (Gal 5:22, Eph 5:9), the fruit of Paul's labor (Rom 1:13, Phil 1:22), and the *fruit* of the readers (Rom 6:21, Phil 1:11). Cooperation, not competition, should characterize believers' relationships, whether on the personal or communal level. For many years, particularly in the late seventies until the middle eighties, the false dichotomy between evangelism and social action was held firmly by many Christian organizations and denominations in Africa. This has changed with many churches and para-church organizations that are now seriously engaged in mercy ministries.

James returns to the theme of partiality, which he previously discussed in 2:1–13. True wisdom is manifested in a life free from partiality or favoritism. True wisdom does not marginalize any person based on race, gender, and color, but instead, it recognizes and affirms the dignity of all humans as those created in the image of God. Wisdom leads to inclusion instead of exclusion. Nepotism, which is rampant in the church as well as in the wider societies in many countries in Africa, is contrary to godly wisdom. In many countries in Africa, there are two systems of justice, one for the rich and the other for the poor. The rich and powerful buy justice, and judges cave under the pressure of the political offices that appointed them. In the church world, leaders can turn blind eyes to the sins of the financial backers. A wise leader must be equitable. The last virtue of wisdom is that it is "without hypocrisy." Unlike hypocrites who pretend to be something they are not, the wise person is sincere.[26] Wisdom is genuine and authentic, and there is no pretending in it.

Verse 18 is pivotal and seems to allude to Matt 5:9, where Jesus pronounces blessedness upon peacemakers: "And the seed whose fruit is righteousness is sown in peace by those who make peace." James has insisted that worldly wisdom leads to strife, disharmony, and disorder; heavenly wisdom brings peace and harmony. Again, James describes wisdom as leading to a holy or moral life. Wisdom is a higher way of living. Peaceable people are wise people, and here James explains that their reward is righteousness. So, righteousness is a result of true wisdom. We once again see the idea of perfection resulting from wisdom. People moving toward perfection understand that an intimate relationship with God requires total loyalty and devotion to God and his word. The quality that expresses the union between God and the Christian is righteousness. God is righteous and calls his people to live righteously. People who allow true wisdom to influence all of their life

26. McKnight, *Letter of James*, 132.

become perfect because they recognize their union with God, and they will enable that relationship to affect all of their decisions and actions.[27] John Wesley comments:

> The principle productive righteousness is sown, like good seed, in the peace of a believer's mind and yields a plentiful harvest of happiness (the fruit of righteousness) for them that make peace—labor to produce this holy peace among all men.[28]

Wesley thus interprets the words as applying to individual peace of mind, an inner experience that characterizes a believer. Such interpretation assumes that verse 18 is independent of the preceding verses. It seems best to understand the passage primarily referring to the community, which has probably been disturbed by jealousy and rivalry. However, both the individual and community aspects are not mutually exclusive. Mitton's observation of the relationship between righteousness and peace here is beneficial:

> In a community, it is only when fair dealing prevails and legitimate grievances are quickly remedied that peace can be maintained. Within the human heart also true peace and lasting peace can only be built upon a foundation of righteousness, that is, obedience to the known will of God.[29]

---

27. Hartin, *Spirituality of Perfection*, 75.

28. Wesley, *Explanatory Notes*, 603.

29. Mitton, *Epistle of James*, 142.

CHAPTER 4

James 4:1–17

IN JAMES CHAPTER 4, James writes about the origins of war, lust, and life's uncertainties. The chapter starts with a challenge to behavior that James saw as proof of ungodly wisdom—fights and quarrels among them. He pondered why people lust and fight over things and still cannot have them. He claimed that the people he was writing to did not have what they wanted because they either did not ask for it or they asked for the wrong thing to satisfy their lust (vv. 1–3). James shows the incompatibility of loving the world and loving God at the same time. He reminded them that the Scriptures claim that the flesh is full of lust and envy, but God has abundant grace and will always give it to people who practice humility. At the same time, God will reject proud people. James urged his readers to submit to God and oppose the devil because the devil will run away from them if they do. Instead, he wanted people to draw closer to God and cleanse their minds and bodies of sin. If they stop their revelry and become humble, James said God would draw near them (vv. 4–6). How believers should treat one another is a matter of importance to James. So, he urged his readers not to speak ill of each other. A person who speaks ill of his brother and harshly judges him is judging the law and taking the place of God, who is the ultimate giver of the law (vv. 7–12). The chapter ends with a warning from James for those who seemed to be sure of their lives. He said nobody could be certain of what would happen to them in the future because they are not in control. So, he cautions believers to consider the Lord's will when making plans because our time on earth is short, and God's will prevails. Thus, he reminded his readers that their lives are temporary and dependent on the will of God.

James then told his readers that to revel and boast the way they do was evil, and to know what good is and not do it is a sin (vv. 13–17).

VERSES 1–3

What is the source of quarrels and conflicts among you? Is not the source your pleasures that wage war in your members?
You lust and do not have; so you commit murder. You are envious and cannot obtain; so you fight and quarrel. You do not have because you do not ask.
You ask and do not receive, because you ask with wrong motives, so that you may spend it on your pleasures.

In his characteristic fashion, James introduces the section with a rhetorical question, which he proceeds to answer himself: interpersonal quarrels and conflicts arise from the unruly passions within each party. The question appears to follow directly on James's expressed concern for peacemaking in 3:18. Returning to his querying of his readers (cf. 3:13), James turned their attention instantly upon the conflicts and disputes among them. He uses three related words: "quarrels," "conflict," and "war."

The first conflict word is "quarrels" (*polemoi*, "wars"). The word can be used for feuds, disagreements, and disputes between families and individuals. In the New Testament, the term often has an apocalyptic flavor. Jesus uses it when speaking of the end times (Matt 24:6, Mark 13:7, Luke 21:9). It appears once in the Pauline Epistles as part of an analogy that draws upon real military practice (1 Cor 14:8) and once in Hebrews to speak of military conflicts won by people "by faith" (11:34). Revelation uses it eight times. Its usage in James as a reference James to small-scale, interpersonal conflict is unique. The second word is *conflicts* (*machai*, "quarrels," "strife," "disputes'). Outside of James, only Paul uses this word in the New Testament in the sense of a personal quarrel (2 Cor 7:5, 2 Tim 2:23, Titus 3:9). That is also the sense in the Septuagint, where it depicts "quarreling" between family and acquaintances (Gen 13:6; see Prov 15:18). Instead of peace and the fruit of righteousness, James's audience was manifesting just the opposite: they were full of mutual oppositions and attacks. Its source is the pleasures that wage war in their members. The third conflict word derives from "soldier" (*strateuma*). Base "sensual pleasures" wage war against the higher moral principles within. These "sensual pleasures" cause problems within the community and battle (*strateuomenōn*) within the person.

As an African adage goes, "*Kokoro to n je efo, inu efo lowa*": the bug eating and destroying the vegetable lives inside it. An antagonist is always "within." In the case of James's readers, this would refer to the members of the community. It is a caution to beware of the enemy inside rather than focus on the outside. Changing the figure somewhat is like the story of a tree that survived harsh weather and wildfires but was eventually destroyed by termites working on it for a long time from within. Within an African context, wars and most tensions always arise from "within"—between ethnic groups and within the state. The presence of disputes and conflicts among persons over particular issues and selfish interests is well known.

James identifies it as the cause of contention in the community (vv. 1, 3). The quarrels and conflicts result from the selfish pursuit of pleasures (*hēdonōn*, "sensual pleasures"). This word is stronger than desires (*epithymia*). In most cases, it has negative connotations, even in Greek literature, and refers to the gratification of the flesh. In the New Testament, it refers only to physical pleasures (Luke 8:14, Titus 3:3, 2 Pet 2:13). James's point is, do not look elsewhere for the source of your conflicts. Look within! The source is selfishness! Two selfish people dig in their heels and accuse each other of causing the problems. Often, others take sides until an all-out war results. But James takes it back to the root cause: selfishness. In sum, James says that conflict will persist until they correctly identify its source.

The phrase "in your members" (NASB) is challenging to translate. The pronoun "your" is plural, showing that James addresses a group of people. But he uses the word "members" (*melesin*), a term referring to the actual limbs of the body. But we can also use metaphorically it for members of a community (Rom 12:5; 1 Cor 12:27; Eph 4:25, 5:30). The visible inter-community conflict reflects the invisible inner conflict within individuals caused by their desires for *sensual pleasures.*[1]

These destructive desires exist among Christians because they do not seek God for their needs ("you do not ask"). They failed to make their desires a matter of prayer. James reminds us of the incredible power of prayer and why believers may live unnecessarily as spiritual paupers—simply because they do not pray or do not "ask" when they pray. James already used the Greek word *aiteo* in 1:5–8. It means to ask for something or make a petition. It implies asking with a sense of urgency and conveys the sense of pleading, begging, imploring.

James cautions, however, that one must have the right motivation for praying. It would not do to seek from God those things that would only serve to satisfy self-centered desires and aims—to seek not to please God better or be more effective in his service, but to gain status over others, comfort, ease, and praise. Like so many "prosperity gospel" preachers in Africa

---

1. Serrão, *James*, 136.

(and elsewhere), they want to use God's provisions, money, leisure, and the like to satisfy themselves. They do this by erecting mansions, purchasing expensive automobiles, acquiring airplanes, not for the greater glory of God but for their own ends and pleasure. Believers must remember that the purpose of prayer is not to satisfy our selfish longings, gratify our desires, or persuade a reluctant God to do our bidding. Instead, the purpose of prayer is to align our will with his and ask him to accomplish his will in our lives.

VERSES 4-6

You adulteresses, do you not know that friendship with the world is hostility toward God? Therefore whoever wishes to be a friend of the world makes himself an enemy of God
Or do you think that the Scripture speaks to no purpose: "He jealously desires the Spirit which He has made to dwell in us"?
But He gives a greater grace. Therefore it says, "God is opposed to the proud, but gives grace to the humble."

Continuing his point, James reminds his hearers that they cannot be friends both of God and the world. An old West African proverb says, "The man who tries to walk two roads will split his pants." That is an apt description of those who try to live for the Lord and the pleasures of this world at the same time. They are trying to walk two roads, which can only lead to disaster in the end. The pursuit of God and self-indulgence at the same time is not possible. Here is an echo of Jesus's words, "you cannot serve God and mammon." Or, as a Tanzanian proverb goes, "two paths defeated the hyena." It is about the story of the greedy hyena that wanted to eat the goat that he saw down on one path and the chicken on the other. It ended up losing both. The author of 1 John makes the same observation (1 John 2:15-17).

James addresses his audience as "adulteresses." This term would ring a bell to the Jewish Christians to whom James addresses the letter. The Old Testament designates Israel as the "bride" or "wife" of God (Deut 31:16, Jer 3:20). Within the context of this metaphor, any disloyalty on Israel's part to their covenant with God is characterized as adultery. So, any group among Israel who took God's laws for granted and carelessly disobeyed them could be denounced, as in the words of Jesus, as "an evil and adulterous generation" (Matt 12:39). In Hosea, those by their disobedience "forsook God," despite their covenant to him, are said to be "playing the harlot." Perhaps James still has the double-souled person in mind (Jas 1:8). What is required is complete consecration to God. Understood in this way, it calls into question the validity of a Yoruba saying, "*igbagbo o ni ki a ma se oro ile*," that is, "Christianity does not forbid one from participating in a cultural festival or worshipping family idols." Such an idea leads to syncretism.

James 4:4b has been used and abused in Africa. A case in point is Nigeria. As recent as the 1990s, some churches have applied the passage to the instruments used in church worship. For example, when the church orchestra uses instruments like guitar, organ, etc., in worship, they are not considered worldly. However, when the church uses local, traditional drums such as *gangan* and *bata*, some Christian denominations and groups consider them not only worldly but also, sometimes, seen as idolatrous. This is because idol worshipers use the same instruments during festivals. However, it is important to say that both the Western and local musical instruments are amoral. The passage has been used to preach against any form of celebration considered "unspiritual," e.g., birthday celebrations, naming ceremonies, and other cultural practices. Close association and mutual interests are the basis of friendship. The Old Testament prophet Amos asked, "Can two walk together, except they are agreed?" (Amos 3:3). To be friendly with the world means to cherish a relation of mutual appreciation with unbelievers, with those who exclude God from their lives, value approval, and goodwill, and be ready either to disguise or outrightly forgo loyalty to God. James called believers to "choose single-minded commitment to God rather than being 'double-minded' and trying to 'have it both ways.'"[2]

The "world" (*kosmos*), must be understood in its broad sense as comprehending not only the people but also the pleasures, riches, and honors of the world. To draw the precise limits of what is called "the friendship" of the world is not so easy.[3]It is the system that humans have built (a tower of Babel) up for themselves to satisfy the lust of the eyes, the lust of the flesh, and the pride of life. The system seeks to exclude God from its thoughts, planning, and living. It may be the world of art, culture, education, science, or even religion.[4] James shares the same outlook about believers' relationship with the world with Paul's and John's exhortations in 2 Cor 6:14–18 and 1 John 2:15–17, respectively:

> Do not be bound together with unbelievers; for what partnership have righteousness and lawlessness, or what fellowship has light with darkness? Or what harmony has Christ with Belial, or what has a believer in common with an unbeliever? Or what

2. David, "Controlling the Tongue and the Wallet," 227.

3. Simeon, *Horae Homileticae*, 87.

4. MacDonald, *Believer's Bible Commentary*, 2236.

agreement has the temple of God with idols? For we are the
temple of the living God; just as God said,
"I WILL DWELL IN THEM AND WALK AMONG THEM;
AND I WILL BE THEIR GOD, AND THEY SHALL BE MY PEOPLE.
"Therefore, COME OUT FROM THEIR MIDST AND BE SEPARATE,"
says the Lord.
"AND DO NOT TOUCH WHAT IS UNCLEAN;
And I will welcome you.
"And I will be a father to you,
And you shall be sons and daughters to Me,"
Says the Lord Almighty. (2 Cor 6:14–18)

Do not love the world nor the things in the world. If anyone
loves the world, the love of the Father is not in him. For all that
is in the world, the lust of the flesh and the desire of the eyes and
the boastful pride of life, is not from the Father, but is from the
world. The world is passing away, and *also* its lusts; but the one
who does the will of God lives forever. (1 John 2:15–17)

The Christian has a choice to make—to please God or the world. Verse
5 builds on James's argument in the preceding verses (vv. 1–4), especially
verse 4. He presented his hearers with a rhetorical question to penetrate
what they were thinking—unwise as it was! Their thinking was misguided
because they had allowed their desires for God and their desires for the
idols of the world to consume them in a total conflict of desire and interpersonal relations.[5] James seemed to have been quoting the Scriptures, but the
Old Testament he mentions is unclear. So is the Spirit's referent—either the
Holy Spirit or human spirit. As Moo rightly says, "in either case, the phrase
reminds us that God has a claim on us by virtue of his work in our lives."[6]
Mitton sums up the point of this verse very well. "God longs the entire,
undivided devotion of the human content. He made it for himself, He has
redeemed it in Christ, and He will not be content so long as any part of it is
handed over to evil. Being God, we cannot satisfy him with only a fragment.
He must have all."[7]

In sharp contrast to the life characterized by envy, jealousy, strife,
and wars, James urges his readers to a life of humility. He cites Prov 3:34
as authoritative support for the claim that Christians should live according to godly wisdom that leads to peace: "God resists the proud but gives
grace to the humble." When we do not become allies of the world but submit

5. Richardson, *James*, 179.
6. Moo, *Letter of James*, 150.
7. Mitton, *Epistle of James*, 156.

ourselves to God and his will for our lives, he will not oppose us but give us grace.

VERSES 7–12

Submit therefore to God. Resist the devil and he will flee from you.
Draw near to God, and He will draw near to you. Cleanse your hands, you sinners; and purify your hearts, you double-minded.
Be miserable and mourn and weep; let your laughter be turned into mourning and your joy to gloom.
Humble yourselves in the presence of the Lord, and He will exalt you.
Do not speak against one another, brethren. He who speaks against a brother or judges his brother, speaks against the law and judges the law; but if you judge the law, you are not a doer of the law but a judge of it.
There is only one Lawgiver and Judge, the One who is able to save and to destroy; but who are you who judge your neighbor?

In the previous section (vv. 4–6), James asked critical questions and provided answers that put his audience on the defensive mode. He now changes his tone and speaks with encouragement about what his readers had to do and the change they had to make to get their lives back on track. The particle "therefore" (*oun*) introduces a series of commands in verses 7–10 in response to Proverbs 3:34 quotation in verse 6.[8] It moves the reader from an exposition that God gives grace to the humble (4:6) to an appeal to be humble.[9] James was giving his readers more than a mere list.

Together, James's instructions in verses 7–10 were intended to be a course correction enabled by the Spirit (v. 5). James issues two commands. First, the believer must submit to God (v. 7a). To "submit" (*hypotagēte*) is a passive form of the verb "subject" or "subordinate." Thus, it means "become subject," "subject oneself," or "obey." In the New Testament, it often refers to voluntary submission, as here. To be submissive is to trust and obey the one to whom one submits.[10] It is a military term that means "get into your proper rank." Second, in verse 7b, James calls for resistance to the devil. The verb "resist" (*antistēte*) means "oppose, set oneself against, . . . to be resistant to power, resist." This verb also occurs in 1 Pet 5:9 in a similar context of resisting the devil (see Eph 4:27, 6:11; 1 Tim 3:6–7). Verse 7b

8. Vlachos, *James*, 142.
9. Vlachos, *James*, 142.
10. Serrão, *James*, 144.

is notably important among African readers whose notion of the "devil" differs significantly from that of the Western world. It is more than a call to humility. African Christians understand it as a call to spiritual warfare. In a continent where calamities, disasters, infant mortality, and various conditions are often associated with spiritual causes, resisting the devil becomes a matter of life and death. Pentecostals, in particular, deem it essential to keep on fighting Satan, who is believed to be operating in the guise of traditional spirits and demonic powers. A central feature of the worldview (cosmology) of many Pentecostal and indigenous churches in Africa is the heartfelt belief that evil, hostile spiritual beings exert a real influence on the physical realm. Much of the liturgy of these churches centers on the spiritual conflict between believers and demonic forces. Hence, the imperative of resisting the devil is a staple of African Christianity.

James does not call for mild resistance. Satan does not deserve the believer's respect. On the one hand, he is not to be accorded any misguided courtesy; on the other hand, he is not to be treated with neutral indifference. Christians must face the devil with determined defiance. Resistance means taking sides, speaking out against the adversary, and strategizing to foil his sinister plots. This resistance is not in human strength alone. James's command comes with a promise of victory: the devil will flee. The devil will not just walk away; he escapes as fast as he can.[11] There is an echo of this verse in a popular chorus sung by African Christians:

> In the name of Jesus (2x)
> We have the victory
> In the name of Jesus (2x)
> Satan will have to flee
> When we stand in the name of Jesus,
> Tell me who has the power to oppose
> In the mighty name of Jesus
> We have the victory.

James gives more commands in verse 8. First, he calls his readers to draw near to God. It is a call that is opposite and complementary to resisting the devil. The call to the readers echoes God's call to Moses and the priests to approach him (Exod 24:2 and 19:22). James uses the imperative form of the verb *engizō* (draw near, come near), a word that suggests God's desire for a close and intimate relationship with his people. He follows the command with another promise: God will draw near them. James is not suggesting a *quid pro quo* action, as is common among many people. Instead, James suggests a mutual relationship with God.

11. Serrão, *James*, 144.

Second, James calls for the cleansing of hands and the purification of hearts. What is true of the Israelites holds for James's readers—sin is a hindrance to approaching God (Exod 19:21–22). "Cleansing hands and hearts" (4:8) applies the language of ritual purity to moral issues, just as 1:27 did when it enjoined keeping oneself "unstained by the world."[12] James is calling for inward repentance. Using the symbolism of hands and heart suggests that every aspect of the believer's life is to be touched. This is like Paul's exhortation in 2 Corinthians 7:1: "therefore having these promises, beloved, let us cleanse ourselves from all defilement of flesh and spirit, perfecting holiness in fear of God." To draw near to God, people must prepare themselves, even as the psalmist affirmed that those who would be close to God must have "clean hands and a pure heart" (Ps 24:4). The prophet Isaiah called to the children of Israel in the same manner (Isa 1:16). Those who come to God must do so in contrition. Faith must show itself in "works."

James's call to cleansing in verse 8b will, no doubt, ring a bell for traditional Africans as they are not only familiar with purification rites but understand the underlying reasons for such acts. Various kinds of purification rites in Africa are tied to multiple events and different reasons.[13] Although not all purification rites are done for religious purposes, religious purification rites are concerned explicitly with each society's relationship with the deity. There are three significant grounds for purification: taboos, the holiness of God, and relationship with the deity. Africans understand purification as "a positive approach to the cleaning and removal of sin and pollution. It involves an outward act that is believed to have an inner spiritual cleansing. The cleansing may be of the body, or a thing or a territory or community."[14] If a diviner makes one aware that they have committed an offense that has resulted in the disruption of their peace, they will have to undergo a ritual cleansing. It may include ritual shaving the hair and bathing in a flowing stream. The sinner undertakes the "washing off" of stains under a priest's guidance on an appointed date, time, and place. The sinner provides what the priest directs them to bring for the "washing." The entire event is symbolic and dramatic. Sin is portrayed as a stain and a filthy rag that can be washed off and cast off, respectively. The removal of sin brings new life just as the rejuvenated person takes on a clean white cloth and casts off the old one.

For James, God's nearness can be experienced by any believer who shows genuine repentance for sin. The demand for authentic and deep

---

12. Blomberg and Kamell, *James*, 183.

13. Ray, *African Traditional Religions*, 90–100.

14. Awolalu, "Sin and Its Removal," 284.

repentance is to be treated seriously, rather than with a casual and light-hearted attitude (v. 9). Drawing near God demands humility (v. 10), returning to the theme of verse 6. Humbling oneself before God involves not only a recognition of his majesty and his aversion to evil (Hab 1:13, but an awareness of one's unworthiness to approach him based on any personal merit. It is the exact opposite of, and the antidote to, the attitude of jealousy and pride that James mentioned in 3:13–14. James's exhortation to humility recalls Jesus's words: "Whoever exalts himself shall be humbled, and whoever humbles himself shall be exalted" (Matt 23:12).

In verses 11–12, James turns back to the matter of speech, a subject of great importance in the letter (1:19, 26; 3:1–12). His call to humility is immediately followed by a warning against slander. That the Scriptures consider slander an egregious sin is without a doubt. Slanderers presume that they know better than God, and judge others by the law while they themselves disobey it. James speaks to the members of the community to avoid speaking against one another. The Greek word, *katalalein*, means "to speak against, to accuse someone," with a suggestion of the false and exaggerated: "to calumniate."[15] It occurs twice in 1 Peter (2:13, 3:16) in the context of the defamation and misrepresentation that Christians suffer from non-Christians. The noun form of the word appears on the list of the practices associated with sinners in Rom 1:30. In practice, in most cases it involves a"talk against another" when the person is not there to defend himself or herself, that is, when a person speaks evil or make derogatory remarks about others behind their back. It is related to gossip and backbiting. For James, slander is contrary to the nature of the community, termed as brothers and sisters. Slander is an intentional spread of distorted information that seeks to discredit another person that results in the tarnishing of the slandered person's reputation. Disparaging a person is, in effect, passing judgment on a brother or sister. A Mozambican proverb says that "slander by the stream will be heard by the frogs," to make the point that when one slanders another person secretly it is self-delusion to think that it will not be eventually made public. A slanderer can be compared to the "Kishi" in Angolan folklore: the Kishi is a horrifying, fast hill-dwelling creature or demon that, according to legend, is two-faced. They have an attractive human face (male) on the front of the body and a hyena's face on the back. The hyena's face has long, sharp teeth and jaws so strong they cannot be pulled off anything it bites. They use their human face and smooth talk, and other charms to attract young women, who they then eat with the hyena face. A slanderer is not only a hypocrite but also a dangerous person to be avoided.

15. Kittel, s.v. "Λαλέω," 602.

VERSES 13–17

Come now, you who say, "Today or tomorrow we will go to such and such a city, and spend a year there and engage in business and make a profit."
Yet you do not know what your life will be like tomorrow. You are just a vapor that appears for a little while and then vanishes away.
Instead, you ought to say, "If the Lord wills, we will live and also do this or that."
But as it is, you boast in your arrogance; all such boasting is evil.
Therefore, to one who knows the right thing to do and does not do it, to him it is sin.

The temptation to live in the moment, celebrate our accomplishments, go through the motions of work, and not worry much about the need of others, or even consider our future (v. 13) is as real today as it was to the readers of James. But as a Yoruba maxim goes, *Eda t'o m'ola kosi* ("Nobody knows tomorrow"). It is a saying that well sums up this section. Although verse 13 probably refers to business people in James's day, its application is just as clear to all planning today. Planning, as such, is not the problem; rather the problem is the attitude by which we make plans for the future in complete self-confidence that everything will go according to plan and work out in the way we want. The problem arises when the will of God is left out of all consideration. In such cases, people give their plans the place that belongs to divine providence and lay aside any element of dependence on the Lord and a realistic evaluation of their limitations. James argues that such an attitude is self-deceptive. James speaks fully in line with the Jewish wisdom tradition on this point. Proverbs warns us of the folly of such an attitude with brutal simplicity: "To man belong the plans of the heart, but from the Lord comes the reply of the tongue" (Prov 16:1). The proverbial maxim, "man proposes but God disposes" echoes in the emptiness of our carnal dreaming: "Do not boast about tomorrow, for you do not know what a day may bring!" (Prov 27:1). Three main issues are apparent in this section. First, God is the source and enabler of the Christian's strength and daily life activities. There must be a total dependence on him. People's lives, mental abilities, talents, and gifts are all from God. Boasting or bragging, an attitude of self-confidence and self-congratulation because of one's capability or intelligence, has no place in anybody's life, especially a follower of Christ. It may find expression in various ways—defiance of God, in disregard for God, and also in the Christian ministry and service for God. Planning one's life without guidance from God is tantamount to ungratefulness and arrogance. When Christians plan their lives without acknowledging God's involvement or asking for his direction, they are ungrateful and disrespectful of the God who is the source of their lives. Their arrogance, manifested in thinking that they are the ones that make things happen, will eventually bring sorrow and pain into their lives.

James's response to the "business plan" of these merchants is like Jesus's response to the rich fool in Luke 12:20: "You fool! This very night your soul is required of you; and now who will own what you have prepared" (NASB). James's warning does not apply only to the rich but to everyone, since neither the poor nor the rich can predict what will happen tomorrow, let alone in the more distant future. The Yoruba have a saying that *Aiye fele*, that is, "life is brittle," a proverb that shows the fickleness and fragility of human life. One should live responsibly and be mindful of the future. Planning without God is foolish and presumptuous and presupposes that God has no say in human affairs. Examples abound of African leaders who have used force to keep them in office and thus made their memory notorious. Some of them accumulated illegal wealth stashed in banks in the West, thinking they would live to enjoy the fruit of their greed and avarice. Nigeria's Sani Abacha, Congo's Joseph Mobutu Sese Seko, Emperor Haile Selassie I (known as the Lion of the tribe of Judah), and Robert Mugabe are examples of African leaders that either died while in office or were overthrown.[16]

Furthermore, in addressing the issue of planning one's life without taking the Lord into serious consideration, James breaks down the false dichotomy between the sacred and secular which parallels the African worldview that does not distinguish between the secular and religious—Africans eat and drink religiously. Today, Christians need to break down the artificial sacred/secular distinctions. They must realize that God is present and needs to be a part of their plans from the beginning. God should not be a "rubber stamp" whose mere function is to sanction whatever believers plan or the decisions they make. They should not make their plans and then ask God to bless them. Second, James recognizes the transitory nature of human life. God has always existed, and in the light of eternity, the few years of our lifetimes are like a blink of an eye. It reinforces James's point that Christians need to ask for God's direction in their lives. He is all-wise and understands what is most important in life.

Third, in verse 17, James seems to sum up what he has discussed so far, namely that failure to do what one knows is good, such as avoiding double-mindedness, shunning partiality, taming one's tongue, humbling

16. There are good examples such as Julius Nyerere of Tanzania, Kenneth Kaunda of Zambia, Goodluck Jonathan of Nigeria, and several others who left office as demanded by law.

oneself, and seeking God's will in life leads to sin. Some people shy away from doing some things because it is not in their personal interests. It is not enough just to avoid doing the wrong things. Christians have to do the right that God expects of them. Actions are a response to God's presence in a Christian's life. They are positive actions that build up the community and make a difference in the world. When Christians do not do what God has prompted them to do, they are as guilty as when they do something they know is wrong.

CHAPTER 5

James 5:1–20

IN JAMES CHAPTER 5, James addresses three specific areas. These include warning the rich oppressors, having patience during struggles, and the prayer of faith. First, in verses 1–6, James addressed those whom he considered guilty of exploitation—using people without giving them their honest day's wage. He noted that many people were being sold into slavery to pay off their debts, and some even died due to starvation. The rich were accumulating wealth at the expense of their workers. James reminded the rich that God sees every deed and he was keeping a record of all their evil. Second, James reminds his readers about the importance of patience. He used the example of a farmer who is patiently waiting for his crop to yield fruits. He mentioned the examples of the perseverance of Job and as they went through various trials. Job persevered during his suffering. He was patient as he was frustrated and fed up with his friends blabbering, yet he still trusted in God.

James told the people not to grumble among each other, or they would be judged. He also said that those who judge others would also be judged and that God is the one true and righteous judge. Third, James does not only encourage but also instructs his audience to not only ask for prayer but also to be available to pray for the sick because they also need prayers. He said that the prayer offered in faith would heal the sick. James asked the people to confess their sins to be forgiven by those they had wronged. James shows the importance of mutual accountability as he urges his audience to realize that it is their responsibility to bring back those who have wandered away from the truth.

VERSES 16

Come now, you rich, weep and howl for your miseries which are coming upon you.
Your riches have rotted and your garments have become moth-eaten.
Your gold and your silver have rusted; and their rust will be a witness against you and will consume your flesh like fire. It is in the last days that you have stored up your treasure.
Behold, the pay of the laborers who mowed your fields, and which has been withheld by you, cries out against you; and the outcry of those who did the harvesting has reached the ears of the Lord of Sabaoth.
You have lived luxuriously on the earth and led a life of wanton pleasure; you have fattened your hearts in a day of slaughter.
You have condemned and put to death the righteous man; he does not resist you.

This section is a scathing denunciation of those who selfishly accumulate riches. Today there are individuals who are wealthier than nations. Using very strong words, James denounces the attitude of those who make their fortunes by exploiting others. More importantly, the rich that are condemned by James are not condemned for the sake of their riches but for the fact that they are not putting their wealth to good use providing for those who are less fortunate. As such, James's accusation of the selfishly rich people is connected to their greed. They hoard money in banks. These rich are saying that they are being shrewd investors, and denying themselves and displaying tremendous industry, but it is all vitiated by self-centeredness. Nigeria is rife with examples of politicians and government officials who bury money in the ground on their farms apart from storing them in European banks where the arms of law cannot reach. Money is kept at the expense of workers. They have taken advantage of people. They have paid them a pittance, and sometimes they have failed to pay them anything. You can imagine these little people turning up in church on the Lord's Day in their rags, aching with hunger, weary from having spent the last week working long hours in backbreaking toil for next to nothing. It is happening today all over the world, the exploitation of the poor and vulnerable, including women and children. In South Africa, for example, investigations revealed noncompliance with government regulations. Here is part of the report:

> Non-compliance with the law by some Mpumalanga security companies has led to guards being exploited by their employers, the Department of Labour has found. The department

discovered that out of 55 private security companies operating in the province, only 23 complied with implementing labour laws, while 22 others failed to obey them. It said some companies were not issuing workers with payslips or failed to pay annual bonuses. About R432,187 was owed to employees due to underpayment and non-payment of annual bonuses. All non-complaint companies were given 14 days to comply or face confirmatory notices.

A week-long inspection blitz by the department last week uncovered non-compliance by some companies through its investigations into the implementation of the National Minimum Wage (NMW) Act, the Unemployment Insurance Fund (UIF) Act, and sectoral determination. The department's acting spokesperson, Makhosonke Buthelezi, said inspectors found 14 employers had contravened the UIF Act by not declaring their employees to the fund as required. Buthelezi added 15 companies had failed to comply with the provisions of the department's sectoral determination, which is the basic condition of employment for employees in a sector or area. It also regulates minimum wages. Seven companies were found to be not complying with the NMW Act.[1]

Salary payment is irregular and there are cases where workers have not been paid for over a year. The salaries of the workers are diverted to personal and private use of a few persons in authority. Although Nigeria is an exporter of oil, fuel shortages persist because the petroleum products are hoarded or diverted to places where the marketers would sell them in what is known as "black markets" at exorbitant prices. Arguably, Nigeria is the largest oil producer in Africa and the sixth in the world. On average, the country produced about two million barrels of crude oil in a day. This volume of oil produced daily in Nigeria is produced majorly in the Niger Delta region of the country that constitutes just about 7 percent of the total land mass of the country. Large oil corporations can be complicit in the exploitation of workers. A report in 2018 shows how Shell, the biggest foreign multinational oil company in Nigeria, earning an estimated US$4 billion from Africa's largest oil producing country in 2017, treats its workers.

A new report from a fact-finding mission by IndustriALL Global Union has revealed the shocking exploitation of contract workers at Shell oil and gas operations in Nigeria. The report documents poverty wages, abuse through contracts, fundamental human right violations, poor health care, health and safety

1. Business & Human Rights Centre, "So. Africa: Labour Department," para. 1–2.

hazards and miserable living condition of Shell's Nigerian workers. "We work like an elephant and eat like an ant," said a worker at the Umuebulu-Etche Flow Station in the outskirts of Port Harcourt. "Our salary at (contractor) Plantgeria is about 95,000 naira (US$257). In Nigeria today, you can't do anything on that. You can't pay your children's school fees. You can't eat well. You can't do anything better for yourself."

Salaries among the workers ranged from US$137 to US$257 per month, working 12 hours a day, six days a week. Some workers said that they had not been paid by their contractors for several months. "If you ask for a pay rise, you will be escorted out by police. And then your job is finished."[2]

Several sub-Saharan African countries have been ruined by criminal dictators such as Bokassa, Mobutu, Abacha, Eyadema, Mugabe—the list goes on and on!—who shifted much of the national wealth to their own Swiss bank accounts. In those countries children who go to church die of malnutrition because of such wickedness. Most Africans live in a culture of lobbyism and cronyism, of spin and sympathy, where politics has become too much an exercise of the exchange of the favors of power. The rich live in sumptuous luxury. "You have lived on earth in luxury and self-indulgence. You have fattened yourselves in the day of slaughter" (v. 5). What a vivid picture! James is referring to people who must have a new car every year, who are weary of their expensive clothes after they have worn them a couple of times. The Christian church has its share of charlatans who use religion to make themselves rich. They vaunt their wealth and compete over who has the biggest jet plane. In a letter appealing for funds to enable him to send materials to the majority world, a preacher writes:

> There is no better way to ensure your own financial security than to plant some seed-money in God's work. His law of sowing and reaping guarantees you a harvest of much more than you sow . . . Have you limited God to your present income, business, house or car? There's no limit to God's plenty! . . . Write on the enclosed slip what you need from God—the salvation of a loved one, healing, a raise in pay, a better job, newer car or home, sale or purchase of property, guidance in business or investment . . . whatever you need . . . Enclose your slip with your seed-money . . . Expect God's material blessings in return . . .[3]

---

2. IndustriALL, "Exploitation of Shell workers in Nigeria," para. 1–4.

3. Stott, *Issues Facing Christians Today*, 226.

The rich murder the innocent. "You have condemned and murdered innocent men, who were not opposing you" (v. 6). Wealth is power. Keeping wealth means keeping power, and so it easily leads to violence. Powerful men use legal processes and are able to condemn the innocent. And the innocent ones do not resist. It is not that they could not or ought not to have resisted their powerful accusers but that they chose not to. First, it is an exercise in futility but, secondly and more importantly, they have committed their souls to the righteous Judge who will reveal all things in that great day. In the following verses James turns his attention from the "rich" whose heartless conduct he has condemned and addresses the believers who are the victims of oppression and ill treatment. He speaks to them words of comfort and encouragement in the face of the humiliation they are suffering, admonishing them to be patient even though he is aware of the bitterness and frustration that may result.

VERSES 7–11

Therefore be patient, brethren, until the coming of the Lord. The farmer waits for the precious produce of the soil, being patient about it, until it gets the early and late rains.
You too be patient; strengthen your hearts, for the coming of the Lord is near.
Do not complain, brethren, against one another, so that you yourselves may not be judged; behold, the Judge is standing right at the door.
As an example, brethren, of suffering and patience, take the prophets who spoke in the name of the Lord.
We count those blessed who endured. You have heard of the endurance of Job and have seen the outcome of the Lord's dealings, that the Lord is full of compassion and is merciful.

In this section James urges his audience to exercise patience and endurance in times of trials. Here he uses the verb *makrothymeo* to urge patience, a word that is commonly used for bearing with people with whom we find difficult and irritating, instead of *hypomeno* which refers to patience in the sense of courageously facing discouraging circumstances. In this paragraph, the two words function as synonyms (James will use the latter word group in verse 11). James uses the coming of the Lord, which he sees as near, as a motivation for them to exercise patience. Here one sees a connection between suffering and eschatological hope that characterize the African Christian. Although Africans are enthused with the possibility of a good life "below" and entertain eschatological views that are decidedly this-worldly, they nevertheless also have a hope for the "above," that is in the future. In contrast to the grim and hopeless picture of Africa painted by *The Economist* in the year 2000, Olapade, a Nigerian American, came to the conclusion that Africa is indeed a continent filled with hope after she undertook an extensive tour of sub-Saharan Africa.[4] She observed that in spite of the everyday challengers and difficulties they face, Africans are resilient, joyful, and innovative. For the African there is always hope. James uses an agricultural metaphor, something which is much at home with ordinary readers in Africa, to drive home his point (4:7b). We have already looked at African resilience in connection with James 1.

Perhaps there is not a Bible character that embodies such a characteristic as Job. So, here, James used Job as a prime example of patience in suffering because of the situation of James's readers. Job's patience stands out because his story is extreme in the amount of pain he endured. Job lost all of his children and his wealth in a single day. He then was covered in painful sores, and his wife offered him no support—she encouraged him to give up, curse God, and die (Job 2:9). When Job's three friends came to comfort him, they could not even recognize him from a distance (Job 2:12). Adding to Job's pain, his friends falsely accused him of wrongdoing and blamed his troubles on his unrepentant heart. Through it all, Job patiently endured (Job 2:10). Although not an African himself, but having lived and served as a missionary in Equatorial Guinea for several years and reading the book of Job through African eyes, Carter gives examples of how African readers readily identify with Job's situation. He tells the story of a Pentecostal pastor, Gregorio, who lost his six-year-old son and found himself accused by his neighbors and church members of sacrificing his child to advance his ministry. In the course of his ministerial studies in a local seminary, Gregorio undertook a classroom assignment in which students were instructed to compose a letter to Job, reflecting their own experiences and understanding of the book. The following is Gregorio's Letter to Brother Job from Equatorial Guinea:[5]

> Brother Job,
>   Each time that I read the Scriptures and meditate on your afflictions and the complaints and accusations that your friends made against you, I ask myself if you have been reincarnated in me. . . . When I look at the situation around me in the land that saw me born, Equatorial Guinea, I can say that it's a photocopy of you.

4. *The Economist*, "Hopeless Africa."
5. Carter, *Inside the Whirlwind*, 167.

The truth is that the world is unjust. Just like you, I passed through three horrible years in which I lost two of my children. One died through an illness. After his death, people from the outside, including my own relatives, said that it was through the witchcraft of my wife's family. We almost separated. The other child (six years old) died in a fire in which there was not a chance to remove even one single belonging from the house. . . . The people attributed the fire to my wife being irresponsible, others affirmed that it was a punishment of God against us because we had done something bad—that God had paid us back with his just judgment. Another group said that we had handed over our children as [witchcraft] sacrifices in our churches. My own heart told me: "Where is the God that you serve and how is it that he allowed you to pass through all of this?"

My country is being devastated with all types of epidemics, sicknesses whose origins are still undiscovered, and horrible deaths. But every time that a person suffers from these things, the idea of others is always that the victims have to confess what they have done. . . . I can almost say that the reasoning of your three friends is typical in my culture. All suffering here is linked to witchcraft or to a sin for which God is judging the person or all the family. There is a famous phrase used in my culture: "God punishes without a stick." I have listened to people lament and cry, saying: "If God exists, why has he permitted this? I don't deserve it, it's not fair!" Others have even taken their lives to prevent further suffering.

In short, this is what we live with every day. With the death of innocent children . . . people who have studied but live poor without jobs, people that suffer sicknesses without knowing where it comes from. Nevertheless, many criminals appear increasingly successful in life. Job, I admire your courage and your mature attitude in responding to your wife and your integrity. Despite everything, you didn't blaspheme against God in all of that (2:9–10). I admire your humble response to God. It's true that the way in which many can demonstrate wisdom is to be silent when the cause is unknown—and not open one's mouth to speak foolishness or falsely accuse the victims.

At least you managed to see restoration in this life. I don't know if Equatorial Guinea and I, if we will have the same grace. Or, perhaps we will have to wait until the redemption of our body when the Lord comes in glory.

Your story truly gives me hope. It gives me the feeling that while man lives on the earth, there is no guarantee that he will not suffer, however innocent or righteous he may be. I wish that everyone could learn from you.

Sincerely,
Your brother Gregorio Nsomboro

In the same manner that James offers his immediate audience hope, it does so to the African reader. While other accounts may say something to the contrary, Africa is a continent of hope.

VERSE 12

But above all, my brethren, do not swear, either by heaven or by earth or with any other oath; but your yes is to be yes, and your no, no, so that you may not fall under judgment.

The background of James's instructions here is obviously Jesus's words in the Sermon on the Mount in Matthew:

> Again, you have heard that it was said to the people long ago, 'Do not break your oath, but keep the oaths you have made to the Lord.' But I tell you, Do not swear at all: either by heaven, for it is God's throne; or by the earth, for it is his footstool; or by Jerusalem, for it is the city of the Great King. And do not swear by your head, for you cannot make even one hair white or black. Simply let your 'Yes' be 'Yes,' and your 'No,' 'No'; anything beyond this comes from the evil one. (Matt 5:33–37)

The importance of this verse within the African context cannot be overstated. Some African denominations understand the verse as forbidding all types of oaths, ranging from the simplest act of declaring one's birth before a judicial officer to a more important act as taking an oath of office. As such, this passage is often used to warn off oaths of any kind. However, on a mundane level, what if one were asked to appear in court contesting a traffic violation, should such a person swear to tell the truth, the whole truth, and nothing but the truth? There are some Christians who, on the basis of our text, refuse to do so. Are they right? Or think of professional oaths, marriage vows, and how even in a civil marriage there is a solemnity about those official promises. Legally, whether a person has made a vow in church calling on God's name or simply made his or her promises before the representative of the state, what he or she has said is treated equally seriously. One cannot dismiss them as "just sounds: mere vocables." As Walters rightly states:

It's becoming increasingly clear that simple honesty and truth telling run unmistakably counter to modern culture. James's conviction is that the Jewish-Christian communities to whom he writes should be places where words *do* matter and where truth is a way of life, not an exception that has to be noted by the invocation of some special "truth-telling formula." He urges his readers to be the kind of people who simply mean what they say, apart from any dramatic appeal to oaths. Failing to be that kind of people betrays an inability to understand the nature of true religion. It also betrays the fundamental impiety of our lives where we act as if God isn't present when we play the cultural games of "acceptable" dishonesty.[6]

VERSE 13

Is anyone among you suffering? Then he must pray. Is anyone cheerful? He is to sing praises.

In the previous section James has counselled his audience to exercise patience in times of suffering. To show that it is not a matter of if but when, James asks a question, "is anyone among you suffering?" In 1:5, he admonished his audience to pray for wisdom in times of trial. Here, he expands his teaching on prayer. Christians are to pray not only to pray for wisdom in times of trial but also for help or deliverance in times of hardships and suffering. This verse resonates with African Christians, who are undergoing various trials. An African disposition and reliance on prayer is well-expressed by the Nigerian cliché, "the intensity of your prayer depends on the magnitude of your problem." Prayer is a dimension of life in Africa, the disposition of one who believes himself or herself to be in communion with divine reality. African prayer is far from exclusively petitionary, but, since Africans commonly live close to the subsistence level, petition in moments of great crisis or need is frequently the occasion of prayer. The African Christian who does not know where the next meal will come from definitely understands and values the prayer of Jesus, "Give us this day our daily bread," more than those who have access to food stamps. Christians in Africa and Latin America tend to pray more frequently, attend religious services more regularly, and consider religion more important in their lives than Christians elsewhere in the world, according to a recent Pew Research

6. Walters, *James*, 91.

Center study.[7] At the same time, Christians in the United States also have comparatively high levels of commitment to their faith.

Trouble, whether mental or physical, should not so overwhelm the Christian as to reduce him or her to a state of petulance and self-pity. James goes on to encourage those who are cheerful to sing psalms. It is common knowledge that occasions of joy often become the time of carelessness and forgetfulness of God but that should be the time to pause and remember God who is the giver of all life's good gifts and turn to him in praise and thanksgiving. When a Christian is fortunate to be to be happy over any situation in life, he or she must praise the Lord. James's words serve as a rebuke to many African Christians who spend so much money on partying for a successful wedding, a miraculous childbirth, or a promotion or graduation, but then come to church with a paltry sum to "praise the Lord."

VERSES 14–16

Is anyone among you sick? Then he must call for the elders of the church and they are to pray over him, anointing him with oil in the name of the Lord; and the prayer offered in faith will restore the one who is sick, and the Lord will raise him up, and if he has committed sins, they will be forgiven him.
Therefore, confess your sins to one another, and pray for one another so that you may be healed. The effective prayer of a righteous man can accomplish much.

James 5:14–16 is arguably the passage that is most cited and appropriated by African Christians today. The reason is not far-fetched. Africa is a continent where health care is dismal and, thus, the passage provides comfort and hope to millions who do not have access to good health care. Most African Christians would agree that James 5:14–16 speaks about healing, but would debate whether it refers to physical or spiritual healing. Particularly Pentecostal and Charismatic Christians continue to argue for the understanding of the text as limited to spiritual healing. Perhaps representative of the former position is that which is argued based on historico-grammatical grounds by Daniel Dei and Robert Ossei-Bonsu. In conclusion of their position, both state:

> . . . from the foregoing, one may understand the context of James 5:14–16: the renewing of spiritual strength amid suffering. This suffering may be caused by diseases, persecutions, trials, interpersonal conflicts, and sin (both against God and other human

7. Pew Research Center, "Age Gap."

beings). In such situations, James offers directives by which the spiritually weak may gain renewal and restoration. The context, therefore, may be understood primarily as directives for the spiritual restoration of the spiritually weak or wearied. In this vein, James 5:14–16 would suggest five (5) major implications for the present-day Christian (especially in Africa) involved in healing ministries. These are: the sick refers basically to those who are spiritually weak or lacking spiritual strength; the elders who are to be called refer to the overseers or leaders of the faith community and not to some special class of individuals in the same community who possess the gift of healing or some special prowess for caring for the sick; the use of oil would suggest a symbolic use of it as a means of refreshing the spiritually weak; the healing of the spiritually weak is the sole discretion of God; and persons lacking spiritual strength are to confess their sins to God (in the event of direct sins against God) and to one another (in the event that those sins causing the spiritual weakness are against others).[8]

However, these conclusions are only partially correct. First, although the Greek *astheneo* can have both literal and metaphorical meanings, coming on the heels of the word *kakopatheo*[9] in verse 13, the word *astheneo* must be understood as a reference to physical healing. This conclusion is further strengthened by the presence of *tonkamnonta*,[10] "the sick" in verse 15a. It is used in reference to *astheneo* in verse 14a. As such, physical illness is in view here. Second, it is clear from the passage that the main emphasis is on the "prayer of faith": this is clear from the statement, ". . . they are to pray over him, anointing him with oil in the name of the Lord; and the prayer offered in faith will restore the one who is sick" (NASB). Third, the word *sozo* ("save") in this context refers to both physical healing and eschatological deliverance.[11] Moreover, as said earlier, the African view of the human person is wholistic. The dichotomous (body and soul) and trichotomous (body,

8. Dei and Osei-Bonsu, "Confession," 30.

9. In its ordinary sense the word refers to distress, hardships, and misfortunes of life. This is the usage of the word in 5:10.

10. "It is used both in classical and koinē periods in reference to physical weakness as a result of either physical working or sickness. James uses the attributive participle of the verb *kamnein* which, when used intransitively means to be weary/fatigued or ill." See Johnson, *Letter of James*, 332.

11. The word could refer to 1) physical healing, e.g., Matt 9:22; Mark 5:34; Luke 8:48; 2) deliverance from physical danger, Matt 27:39; Mark 15:29; Luke 23:39, 3) eschatological salvation, Matt 16:25; Mark 8:35; Luke 9:24 and 4), God's saving activity, 1 Cor 1:18; Eph 2:8. So also Thomas, *Devils, Disease and Deliverance*, 22.

soul, and spirit) views of the person is un-African. As such, one must note that for the African believer, an understanding of healing that restricts it to a strictly physical or spiritual act is inadequate. It is not a matter of either/ or but, in several cases, both/and. Due to their wholistic approach to heal-ings, Africans see causes, effects, and the need for restoration and healing as interrelated. In this context "save" clearly means primarily the restoration of physical health, but is not limited to it. It is the restoration of the person to wholeness, a total well-being, including the person's relationship with God. Fourth, the authors' claim that the elders may not necessarily refer to those who are special seems to suggest that the call for the elders undermines the role of some who might have some spiritual gift of healing. However, as Thomas argued, reading the passage as a way of circumventing charismatic leaders as Dei and Osei-Bonsu seem to have done is hard to defend.[12]

However, in spite of the foregoing one must agree with Dei and Osei-Bonsu in their understanding of the oil as a symbol as well as the necessity of confession of sin against God and others. This is not only biblical but also takes seriously the African view of sin as a disruption of harmony in relationships between the deity and fellow humans. Hence it is a cause of sickness. James has already made several references to sin and shown that the essence of sin is that it is an offence against God. What is an offence to God may even be what human friends applaud such as the preferential treatment accorded to the rich in chapter 2. However, James does not take for granted that sin is necessarily the cause of sin, but he recognizes that it may be.

In 1977, I attended a leadership meeting of the organization of which I was a part at that time. At the end of one particular session, a brother whom I knew very well had suddenly gone blind during the concluding prayer. Like Saul of Tarsus, he was led out of the meeting. He left the camp and was brought to an apartment where I used to stay. He then sent for our leader who came to pray for him and in the process, he confessed that he was struggling with what he was sure was God's call upon his life. Our pastor laid his hands upon him and his eyesight was restored. God's healing act, in this case, and in so many others, in response to believing prayer, included the forgiveness of sins (disobedience) as well as the restoration of physical eyesight (health). While we must be clear that not all sicknesses are due to sin, lest we fall into the errors of Job's friends, here we also see that God does not only deal with the outward manifestations of an illness, but also with its causes. Although many Pentecostal churches and organizations do not stress the connection between sin and healing there are a few exceptions. An

---

12. Thomas, *Devils, Disease, and Deliverance*, 22.

example is the Apostolic Faith Church in Nigeria that I attended for more than a decade. The church is known particularly for its very strong stance on "divine healing," understood and practiced as healing without medicine. As a matter of fact, the use of medicine was not only regarded as a lack of faith, medical education/practice (including medicine, pharmacy, nursing) by the members was frowned upon and discouraged.[13] The strong view of the church on divine healing is that healing is of divine origin. Therefore, to keep a healthy body one must not only acknowledge the owner of health, namely God, but must be in right relationship with him. The church sees sin and healing as opposing to each other and forgiveness and healing as closely related, even inseparable. Faith takes James 5:14–15 seriously and sees healing as a result of observance of the directives of James. However, only the elders of the church can exercise such functions.

James advocates a three-step process of healing. First, one is to call upon the elders of the church. The verse advocates and legitimizes the ministry of healing in a local church.[14] James's call undoubtedly negates the view of many evangelical Christians in Africa and in the West who, as a result of skepticism, contend that healing is no longer something to expect in the twenty-first century. Nevertheless, healing in Africa is not understood as tangential to the liberation that the gospel of Christ provides. Who are these elders? As Thomas rightly observes, they are likely the "recognized leaders in the church."[15] The elders were responsible for pastoral oversight and spiritual direction. Second, the elder is to pray and anoint the sick with oil. Third, the sick person is to confess his or her sins to the elder. It is important to notice that it is explicitly stated that it is not the oil or anointing by human hands or even the believing prayer which is the healing power. They are at best the means which God uses. It is "the Lord" who will raise the sick person back to health (5:15).

It is important at this point to pay some detailed attention the practice (use and abuse) of anointing with oil in the African context given its importance in contemporary African Christianity. As much as this phenomenon is a popular one, much controversy surrounds the biblical authority for its practice. Some Christian leaders have come out to openly condemn it or to express their skepticism about it. Others also express their indifference,

---

13. I knew people who left their medically related professions because of the stance of the church on the use and practice of medicine. I am not sure on how rigid the church is on those issues today. Events in recent years suggest that the church may have softened its stance.

14. Ishola, *Putting Faith to Work*, 195.

15. Thomas, *Devils, Disease, and Deliverance*, 23.

never trying to use it.[16] Should oil be used in praying for the sick? Does the Scripture approve of it or give authority to its usage? Out of several scriptural passages that users of anointing oil refer to, James 5:14–15 stands out perhaps because it is a major New Testament passage that explicitly mentioned the practice, and is often appealed to. Despite some dissenting voices, anointing with oil is a pervasive and popular phenomenon in Africa.

Writing of the popularity of the phenomenon in Nigeria, Ajibade notes:

> One popular charismatic practice today is that of anointing the sick with oil. The practice is so much cherished that some ministers don't get out of their home without a bottle of olive oil in their pocket or bag. Church members too have made the same olive oil a constant companion as one can see a bottle in their bags, cars, offices, shops, and open places in their homes. Anointing services are popular programs that attract mass attendance and testimonies of healing, and other miracles are shared from time to time in such gatherings. The practice, however, is not limited to Charismatic/Pentecostal circles. The Evangelical and mainline churches are also involved in the use of oil in anointing the sick when praying for them.[17]

It is particularly important to observe that the popularity of the practice is not limited to one stream of Christian tradition in Africa, but cuts across denominational lines. In the same vein, writing of the same phenomenon in Ghana, Asamoah-Gyadu states:

> In Ghana, several handbills, invitation cards, television clips with dramatic scenes of the Spirit in action, radio announcements, wall posters, and street overhead banners, advertise various worship services that culminate with anointing. . . . Anointing services . . . are special worship services during which olive oil is applied to various parts of the body or even sometimes taken orally, in order to effect healing, reverse misfortunes, or empower people for successful living, as the case may be. Olive oils may even, in the case of Pentecostal media preachers, be placed on radios and TV sets during broadcasts in order to mediate infusion with power through the airways.

---

16. Although most of the controversies and skepticism are warranted and may be due to lack of understanding, others arise out of the indiscriminate and unbiblical use of the anointing oil beyond the mandate of James 5:16 as well the New Testament. In such cases, preachers appeal to the Old Testament for the legitimacy of their practices. For the latest discussion of this problem, see Clarke, *Pentecostalism*, 76–107.

17. Ajibade, "Anointing the Sick with Oil," 166.

The oils may then be applied to ailing body parts or be drunk as spiritual prophylactics.[18]

What is the significance of the oil? This is an important question within the African context with varied opinions. There are three basic views among African Pentecostals. First are those who exhibit an attitude of indifference. While they might profess to believe in the use of the anointing oil because it is in the Scriptures and claim to take the Scriptures seriously for what it says, nevertheless they do not follow this practice. This is probably because some of these churches actually witness miracles, healings, and deliverances without the use of the anointing oil. Perhaps their attitude concerning the Lord's Supper also underlies their indifference to the application of oil to the body. In other words, it is possible to surmise that churches in this category are those likely to be opposed to anything that appears ritualistic. The second group comprises those who do not only believe it but actually practice it, although the frequency of use varies in these churches. The third group comprises those who do not only believe or practice but actually seem to go far beyond what is written in James. This group, unfortunately, could boast of megachurches and large ministries. Perhaps representative of this view is a prominent Pentecostal leader with one of the largest congregations in Nigeria who once wrote a book titled *The Mystery of the Anointing Oil* where he writes:

> There are mysteries in heaven packaged for the living on earth. The anointing oil is a mystery of the end-time, the unfolding of the manifold wisdom of God . . . The anointing oil is no ritual! It is no magic wand! It is not a symbol! It is not a religious rite or doctrine. It is not a chemical product! It is not oil! It is the Spirit of God, mysteriously packaged in a bottle, mysteriously designed to communicate the power of God, bodily. It is the power of God in your hand, in the person of the Holy Spirit. . . It is the all-purpose drug for all ailments of life. It is the might of God. No gate can close against it. Every gate lifts up at its appearance . . . It is what it takes to be absolutely free. It destroys all discomforts of life. It is God's standard against every invasion of the enemy. It is the carrier of mysterious virtue.[19]

In the same vein, in a message preached titled "Mystery of the Anointing Oil at the Dominion Satellite Fellowship" on August 15, 2012, the preacher says:

18. Asamoah-Gyadu, *Contemporary Pentecostal Christianity*, 235–36.
19. Oyedepo, *Mystery of the Anointing Oil*, 56.

The anointing oil is a mystery of the Kingdom of God. Mysteries are in-explainable, but the results are undeniable. Every time the anointing oil is applied, the Holy Spirit manifests. It is the power of the Holy Spirit mysteriously packaged in a bottle. When the oil is applied the finger of God moves supernaturally to destroy any work of the enemy. It transfers the unlimited power of God to our lives and situations. The enemy cannot touch any person or object the oil is applied to. There is no situation that is above the oil. In order for your situation to be above the oil, it would have to be above the power of the Holy Spirit, and we know that is impossible. Praise God![20]

An aspect of this passage which has been neglected by believers in Africa is that of confession. One wonders if this is a reaction against the mandatory practice of confession to a priest in the Roman Catholic Church as the means of receiving absolution. To use the text in this way is, without a doubt, quite inappropriate. While much has been made of the practice of anointing with oil, African Pentecostals in particular have not as much focused on the importance of confession and its importance for healing. Although the text advocates confession, it does not suggest confession to a priest, either privately or on a weekly basis. Instead, although not limited, confession is between fellow Christians who have been sinned against. Those who shrink from confession would always ask: "Is it not enough for me to confess to God?" Yes, we might answer: If the confession to God brings deliverance from the sense of fighting our battles alone, then it is adequate. But there are times when confession to our fellow human beings becomes the means of total freedom. This is a case of restitution, a doctrine that is still taught by some African denominations such as the Deeper Life Bible Church and The Apostolic Faith. As noted by Onunwa, the meaning and uses of confession cannot be overemphasized, especially considering the effects on the life and health of a patient. He writes:

Many functional disturbances and in the long run many organic lessons are the direct consequences of unresolved remorse and guilt. Some medical practitioners have testified that some long-standing cases of insomnia, palpitations, headaches, a disorder of the digestive organs, and hypertension have disappeared overnight after confessions of a lie or an immoral sex affair. . . . A guilty conscience clogs the flow of vitality and inhibits the joy of a free and open heart. The Igbo of Nigeria who realize the enormity of unconfessed and unrepented sins practice a ritual of Itu-Ogu as a part of the therapy. This ritual is performed before or

20. Freedom Ministries, "Mystery-of-the-Anointing-Oil," para. 1.

during the healing when a patient or his close relative is asked to unburden his heart by confessing his sins before seeking divine blessings. The Bible is clear about the fact that repentance and confession are essential steps towards the health of the soul (Jas. 5: 16; cf. 2 Sam. 24:7; Dan. 9:20; Acts 19:18).[21]

Onunwa's comments about the Igbo tribe in Nigeria highlight the connection of repentance and healing in African society. The fourfold reference to prayer in verses 13–16 is followed by James's general comment that "the effective prayer of a righteous man can accomplish much." An illustration of such prayer is given in the next verse. Elijah's prayer on Mount Carmel has provided one of the foundations for so many "prayer mountains" established by African Christians. Moreover, one always hears African Christians sometimes praying that God will rain down fire from heaven to consume their enemies.

VERSES 17-18

Elijah was a man with a nature like ours, and he prayed earnestly that it would not rain, and it did not rain on the earth for three years and six months. Then he prayed again, and the sky poured rain and the earth produced its fruit.

James gives Elijah as an example of one whose prayers were answered. A popular chorus among African Pentecostals is based on these two verses:

> O Lord send another Elijah to pray Thy power down
> Send the fire, also send the rain,
> To heal the sick, raise the dead, and glorify Thy name
> O Lord I want to be another Elijah here

Elijah was just an ordinary man so far as his feelings and desires were concerned, but how he did pray! God heard Elijah's earnest prayers and stopped the rain for three and a half years. A great famine came upon Israel as punishment for the sins of the people. It was at the top of Mount Carmel that Elijah prayed again to have the rain restored. God desired to put the faith of Elijah to the test, or it may be that God wanted to teach us to hold on in prayer until the answer comes. Elijah had to pray seven times, but the answer came—and how it rained! This writer is a witness to an Elijah-like

---

21. Onunwa, "Biblical Basis for Some Healing Methods in African Traditional Society," 60.

episode that took place in his home town. During a spell of drought believers gathered to pray fervently for God to open the windows of heaven and send rain. The prayer was about to be answered. The heavens were heavy and the cloud was thick and there was a great expectation. At this point a voodoo man came out and started bragging that it was his god (idol) that was about to send down rain. A brother, seeing this and grieved in the spirit, challenged the voodoo man, pointed his hands to the sky, and told him that the rain will not fall that day but it will fall at a particular time the next day. Then the true God will be known. Lo and behold, in a matter of minutes, the clouds were clear and there was no rain. However, the rain fell the next day at the appointed time that the Christian mentioned the previous day and God was glorified.

A common saying in Africa is that "a prayerless Christian is a powerless Christian." How true! African Christians take prayer seriously. The seriousness with which they take it is seen different ways. Overnight prayer meetings are the staple of many Christian organizations and churches. It is also seen in songs and choruses. Here is an example of a popular chorus among African believers that accentuates the importance of prayer.

> *Prayer is the key,*
> *Prayer is the key,*
> *Prayer is the master key.*
> *Jesus started with prayer*
> *And ended with prayer:*
> *Prayer is the master key.*

James's emphasis on righteous prayer is a window into understanding both the prayerlessness and the powerlessness of our day. Many believers have given up on prayer because they have decided either that it does not work or that they are self-sufficient—they can meet their own needs and solve their problems more efficiently without any assistance from God. James addressed such disposition in chapter 4. "The halfhearted prayers of halfhearted people hardly qualify as the kinds of prayers James commends here."[22] If a hurried prayer life is what characterizes our fellowship with God, then we are unlikely to grow in the spiritual maturity we need to serve God.

22. Walters, *James,* 205–6.

VERSES 19–20

My brethren, if any among you strays from the truth and one turns him back,
let him know that he who turns a sinner from the error of his way will save his
soul from death and will cover a multitude of sins.

In these last two verses, James once again demonstrates his pastoral concern by addressing the issue of a believer who strays from the truth, that is,
who has backslidden. He begins his final plea as so many of his earlier ones
by addressing them with his usual familial language, "brothers and sisters"
(*adelphoi*). It is not clear what prompted James's concern. First, in light of
the fact that James's audience was going through fiery trials and persecu-
tions (Jas 1:2), it is possible that some of them might have succumbed to the
pressures of their terrible situation and begun to doubt the goodness of God
(Jas 1:17). In other words, the pain and consistent persecution they were
facing and the delay in getting reprieve from their suffering might not only
have raised serious questions about the goodness of God but also led some
to wander and backslide from the truth. If God is as generous and powerful
as James has portrayed him, why would he not stop the persecution or bring
an end to whatever trial was besetting the believer?

Second, the use of the Greek word, *planaō*, "stray or wander," often
refers to any deviation from the truth of the faith, whether inadvertent or
intentional, minor or major. It refers to major offenses in Matthew 22:29,
24:5; 2 Timothy 3:13; Titus 3:3; and 2 Peter 2:15. In its present context,
James is concerned about those who sincerely want to do right, but have
gone astray. He also shows his perplexity concerning Christians whose actions do not match their profession of faith—"this should not be" (3:10).
For James, correct beliefs must be evidenced in correct behavior. Without
mention of what might have caused a person to wander from the truth,
his admonition presupposes that it is possible for a believer to depart from
the truth, or wax cold in the faith. The "truth" (Greek, *alētheias*) does not
simply refer to Christian doctrine in a narrow sense, but is "the whole code
of religious knowledge and moral precept accessible to the members of the
Christian church. To err from it means any departure from the right path
in thought or conduct."[23] "The truth from which one has wandered is not
just intellectual or doctrinal (though that would be involved); it includes
the practical righteousness indicated by the Hebrew word *ĕmet*, which the
Greek OT usually translates with the word *alētheia*. It encompasses both

---

23. Ropes, *James*, 313.

thought (truth) and deed (fidelity)."[24] The wandering member of the community, whether or not he or she has already left the community of faith, is to be brought back to a faithful walk. The Greek verb translated here as "turns [him] back" (*epistrephēi*) means to turn someone around (Isa 6:10; Acts 3:19). It is a matter of turning back to the faith from which one has strayed. In his appeal for "one" to turn back the erring person, James accentuates the care for one another within the community. It is not only the leaders of the community who are involved in James's instruction, but each individual member. Each member of the Christian community is expected to demonstrate a sense of responsibility for the good of his brother or sister. "If *anyone* among you strays from the truth and one turns him back" emphasizes mutual concern and responsibility for one another through the task of loving doctrinal and moral correction.

In verse 20, James addresses the community on how to deal with the hypothetical situation in verse 19. He reminds us that, while it is possible for anyone to wander from God's truth, it is equally possible to bring such a person back. It is pertinent to note that James does not delegate the task of restoring an erring one to the leader of the community, something which would fit the African communal ethos, but entrusts all with this responsibility. In the same way that the believing community must avoid the temptation of dissociating from the less privileged, poor, and sick, it should not leave the straying believer to his or her ways. Instead, there must be a deliberate effort to restore or turn such a person back. The spiritual condition of a fellow Christian is of concern to the whole community. James asks his readers to join him in this ministry of restoration, the effect of which is the forgiveness of sins and the salvation of the sinner. This verse is best summed up in Proverbs 24:11–12:

> Deliver those who are being taken away to death,
> And those who are staggering to slaughter, Oh hold *them* back.
> If you say, "See, we did not know this,"
> Does He not consider *it* who weighs the hearts?
> And does He not know *it* who keeps your soul?
> And will He not render to man according to his work? (NASB)

24. Serrão, *James*, 188.

BIBLIOGRAPHY

Ajibade, Ezekiel A. "Anointing the Sick with Oil: An Exegetical Study of James 5:14–15." *Ogbomoso Journal of Theology* 13 (2008) 166–77.

Akpan, Chris O. "A Comparative Analysis of Causality in Buddhism and African Philosophy." *International Research Journals Review* 2 (2011) 721–29.

Allison, Dale C., Jr. "Blessing God and Cursing People: James 3:9–10." *Journal Of Biblical Literature* 130 (2011) 397–405.

Asamoah-Gyadu, Kwabena. *Contemporary Pentecostal Christianity: Interpretations from An African Context.* Oxford: Regnum, 2013.

Awolalu, J. O. "Sin and Its Removal in African Traditional Religion." *Journal of the American Academy of Religion* 44 (1976) 275–87.

Baker, William R. "Above All Else": Contexts of the Call for Verbal Integrity in James 5:12." *Journal For the Study Of The New Testament* 54 (1994) 57–71.

Batten, Alicia J. *Friendship and Benefaction in James.* Atlanta: SBL, 2017.

———. "The Jesus Tradition and the Letter of James." *Review and Expositor* 108 (2011) 381–90.

Bauckham, Richard. *James: Wisdom of James, Disciple of Jesus the Sage.* New York: Routledge, 2002.

Bauer, Walter, and Frederick William Danker. *A Greek-English Lexicon of the New Testament and Other Early Christian Literature.* 3rd ed. Chicago: University of Chicago Press, 2000.

Blomberg Craig L., and Mariam J. Kamell. *James.* Zondervan Exegetical Commentary on the New Testament 16. Grand Rapids: Zondervan, 2008

Brosend, William F. *James and Jude.* The New Cambridge Bible Commentary. Cambridge: Cambridge University Press, 2004.

Boyce, James L. "A Mirror of Identity: Implanted Word and Pure Religion in James 1:17–27." *Word and World* 35 (2015) 213–21.

Bratcher, Robert Galveston. "Exegetical Themes in James 3–5." *Review and Expositor* 66 (1969) 403–13.

Bray, Gerald L., ed. *James, 1–2 Peter, John, Jude.* Ancient Christian Commentary on Scripture 11. Downers Grove, IL: InterVarsity, 2000.

Business & Human Rights Centre. "So. Africa: Labour Department Investigation Reveals Exploitation of Workers by Security Companies." https://www. business-humanrights.org/fr/dernières-actualités/so-africa-labour-department-investigation-reveals-exploitation-of-workers-by-security-companies/.

Byron, John. "Living in the Shadow of Cain: Echoes of a Developing Tradition in James 5:1–6." *Novum Testamentum* 48 (2006) 261–74.

Carter, Jason A. *Inside the Whirlwind: The Book of Job through African Eyes*. African Christian Studies Series. Eugene, OR: Pickwick, 2017.

Charles, Ronald. "Rahab: A Righteous Whore." *Neotestamentica* 45 (2011) 206–20.

Chester, Andrew, and Ralph P. Martin. *The Theology of the Letters of James, Peter, and Jude*. Cambridge: Cambridge University Press, 1994.

Church, C. "A 'Complete' Ethics: James' Practical Theology." *Review and Expositor* 108 (2011) 407–15.

———. "James' Theocentric Christianity: An Opportunity for Christian-Muslim Conversation?" *Review and Expositor* 108 (2011) 429–36.

Clarke, Clifton R. *Pentecostalism: Insights from Africa and the African Diaspora*. Eugene, OR: Cascade, 2018.

Crocombe, Jeff. "The Seventh-day Adventist Church in Southern Africa—Race Relations and Apartheid." Paper presented at Association of Seventh-day Adventist Historians, Oakwood College, Huntsville, AL.

Dahir, Abdi Latif. "Joy in Happiness: Some of the World's Most Unhappy Countries Are Also the Most Optimistic." https://qz.com/africa/942184/some-of-the-worlds-most-unhappy-countries-are-also-the-most-optimistic.

David, Peter. *Commentary on James*. New International Greek Testament Commentary. Grand Rapids: Eerdmans, 1982.

———. "Controlling the Tongue and the Wallet: Discipleship in James." In *Patterns of Discipleship in the New Testament*, edited by Richard N. Longenecker, 225–47. Grand Rapids: Eerdmans, 1996.

Davids, P. H. "God and the Human Situation in the Letter of James." *Criswell Theological Review* 8 (2001) 31–43.

Dei, Daniel, and Robert Osei-Bonsu. "Confession, Prayer, and Healing: Rethinking James 5:14–16." *Global Advanced Research Journal of Arts and Humanities* 3 (2015) 28–36.

Dibelius, Martin. *The Epistle of James*. Revised by H. Greeven. Hermeneia. Philadelphia: Fortress, 1975.

Dube, Musa W. "Rahab is Hanging Out a Red Ribbon: One African Woman's Perspective on the Future of Feminist New Testament Scholarship." In *Feminist New Testament Studies*, edited by Kathleen O'Brien Wicker, Althea Spencer Miller, and Musa W. Dube, 177–202. New York: Palgrave Macmillan, 2005.

Duncan, Graham A. "Practical Theology: "Faith Apart from Works is Dead." *Journal Of Theology for Southern Africa* 53 (2000) 47–53.

The Economist. "Hopeless Africa." May 11, 2000. https://www.economist.com/leaders/2000/05/11/hopeless-africa.

Eliot, George. *Mill on the Floss*. Penguin Classics. London: Penguin, 2003.

Elliott-Binns, Leonard E. "James 1:18: Creation or Redemption?" *New Testament Studies* 3 (1957) 148–61.

Ellsworth, Roger. *Opening Up James*. Opening Up Commentary. Leominster: Day One, 2009.

Eyokoba, Sam. "Bakare Replies an Aggrieved Member." https://www.vanguardngr.com /2020/03/bakare-replies-aggrieved-member/.

Evans, Louis H. *A Make Your Faith Work: A Letter from James.* Ada, MI: Fleming Revell, 1957.

Felder, Cain Hope. "Partiality and God's Law: An Exegesis of James 2:1–13." *Journal Of Religious Thought* 39 (1983) 51–69.

————. *Troubling Biblical Waters: Race, Class, and Family.* Maryknoll, NY: Orbis, 1989.

Freedom Ministries. "Mystery-of-the-Anointing-Oil." http://freedomministries.org/wp -content/uploads/2012/08/Fellowship-Aug152012-Mystery-of-the-Anointing-Oil. pdf.

Gaiser, Frederick J. "'Are Any Among You Sick?' The Church's Healing Mandate (James 5:13–20)." *Word and World* 35 (2015) 241–50.

Garland, David E. "Severe Trials, Good Gifts, and Pure Religion: James 1." *Review and Expositor* 83 (1986) 383–94.

Ghantous, Hadi. "Was Job 'Patient'? Is God 'Just'?" *Theological Review* 33 (2012) 22–38.

Gowler, David B. *James Through the Centuries.* Wiley Blackwell Bible Commentaries. Oxford: Wiley Blackwell, 2014.

Green, Joel B. *Reading Scripture as Wesleyans.* Nashville: Abingdon, 2010.

Adewunmi, Bim. "Nigeria: The Happiest Place on Earth." *The Guardian,* January 4, 2011. https://www.theguardian.com/global/2011/jan/04/nigerians-top-optimism-poll.

Guest, Edgar A. *Collected Verse of Edgar A. Guest.* Chicago: The Reilly and Co., 1934.

Gyekye, Kwame. *An Essay in African Philosophical Thought: The Akan Conceptual Scheme.* Rev. ed. Philadelphia: Temple University Press, 1995.

Gylver, Sunniva. "Reading James in Oslo: Reflections on Text, Mission and Preaching." *Currents in Theology and Mission* 41 (2014) 404–11.

Hanks, Tom. *The Subversive Gospel: A New Testament Commentary of Liberation.* Cleveland: The Pilgrim, 2000.

Harris, Joseph. *Africans and Their History.* New York: Meridian, 1998.

Hartin, Patrick J. "'Come Now, You Rich, Weep and Wail . . .' (James 5:1–6)." *Journal Of Theology For Southern Africa* 84 (1993) 57–63.

————. "The Letter of James: Faith Leads to Action (The Indicative Leads to the Imperative)." *Word and World* 35 (2015) 222–30.

————. *James.* Sacra Pagina. Collegeville, MN: Liturgical, 2009.

————. *James and the "Q" Sayings of Jesus.* Library of New Testament Studies. London: Bloomsbury Academic, 2015.

————. *A Spirituality of Perfection: Faith in Action in the Letter of James.* Collegeville, MN: Liturgical, 1999.

Hatch, William Henry Paine. "Note on the Hexameter in James 1:17." *Journal of Biblical Literature* 28 (1909) 149–51.

Hearon, H. E. "'But BE Doers of the Word': Power and Privilege in James." *Encounter* 72 (2011) 81–90.

Hincks, Edward Young. "A Probable Error in the Text of James ii.18." *Journal Of Biblical Literature* 18 (1899) 199–202.

Hoppe, Leslie J. *There Shall Be No Poor Among You.* Nashville: Abingdon, 2004.

Hughes, David M. "The Best Seat in the House: James 2:1–10, 14–17." *Review and Expositor* 97 (2000) 223–27.

Idowu, Bolaji. *African Traditional Religion: A Definition.* Maryknoll, NY: Orbis, 1973.

IndustriALL Global Union. "IndustriALL investigation uncovers exploitation of Shell workers in Nigeria." http://www.industriall-union.org/industriall-investigation-uncovers-exploitation-of-shell-workers-in-nigeria.

Internal Displacement Monitoring Centre. "10 Million People Internally Displaced Across Sub-Saharan Africa in 2018." https://www.internal-displacement.org/global-report/grid2019/downloads/press_releases/2019-grid-pressrelease-africa-en.pdf.

Isaacs, Marie E. "Suffering in the Lives of Christians: James 1:2–19A." *Review and Expositor* 97 (2000) 183–93.

Ishola, Solomon Ademola. *Putting Faith to Work.* Ibadan, Nigeria: Daybis Limited, 2008.

Jackson-McCabe, Matt. "Enduring Temptation: The Structure and Coherence of the Letter of James." *Journal for the Study of the New Testament* 37 (2014) 404–11.

Jastram, Nathan, and William C. Weinrich. "Man as Male and Female: Created in the Image of God." *Concordia Theological Quarterly* 68 (2004) 3–96.

Jenkins, Philip. *The New Faces of Christianity: Believing the Bible in the Global South.* Oxford: Oxford University Press, 2006.

Johnson, Luke Timothy. *James: Introduction, Commentary, and Reflections.* The New Interpreter's Bible 12. Nashville: Abingdon, 1998.

———. *The Letter of James.* Anchor Bible 37A. New York: Doubleday, 1995.

———. "The Mirror of Remembrance (James 1:22–25)." *Catholic Biblical Quarterly* 50 (1988) 632–45.

Kamell, Mariam. "The Implications of Grace for the Ethics of James." *Biblica* 92 (2011) 274–87.

———. "James 1:27 and the Church's Call to Mission and Morals." *Crux* 46 (2010) 15–22.

———. "Review of James through the Centuries." *Themelios* 39 (2014) 544–46.

Keddie, Gordon J. *The Practical Christian: The Message of James.* Welwyn Commentary Series. Darlington, UK: Evangelical, 1989.

Kittel, Gerhard. "Λαλέω." In *Theological Dictionary of the New Testament* 10, edited by Gerhard Kittel et al., 602. Grand Rapids: Eerdmans, 1964.

Komolafe, Abiodun. "As Emir Sanusi Becomes History." https://nigeriaworld.com/articles/2020/mar/141.html.

Laws, Sophie. *The Epistle of James.* Harper's New Testament Commentaries. San Francisco: Harper & Row, 1980.

Lewis, Floyd, Jr. "The Conversation of a Christian." *Theological Educator* 34 (1986) 43–47.

Lockett, D. "Strong and Weak lines: Permeable Boundaries between Church and Culture in the Letter of James." *Review and Expositor* 108 (2011) 391–405.

Longenecker, Richard N., ed. *Patterns of Discipleship in the New Testament.* Grand Rapids: Eerdmans, 1996.

Love-Fordham, April. *James in the Suburbs: A Disorderly Parable of the Epistle of James.* Eugene, OR: Resource, 2014.

MacDonald, William. *Believer's Bible Commentary: Old and New Testaments.* Edited by Arthur Farstad. Nashville: Thomas Nelson, 1995.

Magesa, Laurenti. *African Religion: The Moral Traditions of Abundant Life.* Maryknoll, NY: Orbis, 1997.

Marcus, Joel. "'The Twelve Tribes in the Diaspora' (James 1.1)." *New Testament Studies* 60 (2014) 433–47.

Martin, R. A., and John H. Elliott. *James I, II Peter, Jude.* Augsburg Commentary on the New Testament. Minneapolis: Augsburg, 1982.

Martin, Ralph P. *James.* Word Biblical Commentary 48. Waco, TX: Word, 1988.

Maynard-Reid, Pedrito U. *Poverty and Wealth in James.* Maryknoll, NY: Orbis, 1987.

Mbiti, J. S. *African Religion and Philosophy.* New York: Praeger, 1969.

McCartney, D. G. "Self-Deception in James." *Criswell Theological Review* 8 (2011) 31–43.

McClendon, David. "Sub-Saharan Africa Will Be Home to Growing Shares of the World's Christians and Muslims." https://www.pewresearch.org/fact-tank/2017/04/19/sub-saharan-africa-will-be-home-to-growing-shares-of-the-worlds-christians-and-muslims/.

McKnight, Scot. *The Letter of James.* NICNT. Grand Rapids: Eerdmans, 2011.

Metuh, E. Ikenga. *God and Man in African Religion: A Case Study of the Igbo in Nigeria.* London: Geoffrey Chapman, 1981.

Miller, Andrew. *Internal History of the Church (107 A.D.–245 A.D.)* https://bibletruthpublishers.com/internal-history-of-the-church-107-a-d-245-a-d-chapter-8/millers-church-history/lrc15062–16035.

Mitton, C. Leslie. *The Epistle of James.* Grand Rapids: Eerdmans, 1966.

Montgomery, Bert. "Deaf, Dumb and Blind Churches: James Meets The Who (Jas 2:14–17)." *Review and Expositor* 108 (2011) 439–44.

Moo, Douglas J. *The Letter of James.* The Pillar New Testament Commentary. Grand Rapids: Eerdmans, 2000.

Musopole, Augustine C. *Being Human in Africa: Toward an African Christian Anthropology.* American University Studies 65. New York: Peter Lang, 1994.

Nienhuis, David R., and Robert W. Wall. *Reading the Epistles of James, Peter, John and Jude as Scripture.* Grand Rapids: Eerdmans, 2013.

Nkansah-Obrempong, James. *Foundations for African Theological Ethics.* Carlisle, Cumbria: Langham Monographs, 2013.

Nothwehr, Dawn M. *That They May Be One: Catholic Social Teaching on Racism, Tribalism, and Xenophobia.* New York: Orbis, 2008.

Nwachukwu, Daisy N. "The Christian Widow in African Culture." In *The Will to Arise: Women, Tradition and the Church in Africa,* edited by Mercy Amba Oduyoye and Musimbi R. Kanyoro, 56. Maryknoll, NY: Orbis, 1992.

Nwaigbo, F. "Tribalism Versus Evangelization in Sub-Saharan Africa." *African Ecclesiastical Review* 47 (2005) 131–59.

Ogunyemi, K., et al. "Indigenous African Wisdom and its Orientation to the Common Good: Responsible Leadership and Principled Entrepreneurship." In *Responsible Management in Africa, Volume 1: Traditions of Principled Entrepreneurship,* edited by K. Ogunyemi et al., 1–12. Bingley: Emerald, 2022.

Okoye, James C. "Evangelical Poverty and Culture." *Afer* 31 (1989) 37–54.

Onunwa, Udobata. "Biblical Basis for Some Healing Methods in African Traditional Society." *East Africa Journal of Evangelical Theology* 7 (1988) 56–63.

Osborne, Grant R. "James, 1–2 Peter, Jude." *Cornerstone Biblical Commentary.* Carol Stream, IL: Tyndale House, 2011.

Oyedepo, David O. *The Mystery of the Anointing Oil.* Ikeja, Lagos: Dominion, 1995.

Painter, John. "James as the First Catholic Epistle." *Interpretation* 60 (2006) 245–59.

Painter, John, and David deSilva. *James and Jude.* Paideia Commentary on the New Testament. Grand Rapids: Baker, 2012.

Phifer, Kenneth G. "James 2:1–5." *Interpretation* 36 (1982) 278–82.

Pickar, Charles H. "Is Anyone Sick Among You?" *Catholic Biblical Quarterly* 7 (1945) 165–74.

Perdue, Leo G. "Paraenesis and the Epistle of James." *Zeitschrift für die Neutestamentliche Wissenschaft und die Kunde der Älteren Kirche* 72 (1981) 241–56.

Perkins, Pheme. *First and Second Peter, James, and Jude.* Interpretation. Louisville: John Knox, 1995.

Pew Research Center. "The Age Gap in Religion Around the World." June 13, 2018. https://www.pewresearch.org/religion/2018/06/13/the-age-gap-in-religion-around-the-world/.

Polhill, John B. "Prejudice, Partiality, and Faith: James 2." *Review and Expositor* 83 (1986) 395–404.

Popkes, Wiard. "Two Interpretations of 'Justification' in the New Testament: Reflections on Galatians 2:15–21 and James 2:21–25." *Studia Theologica* 59 (2005) 129–46.

Premium Times. "Tinubu, Fashola clash at birthday colloquium." https://www.premium timesng.com/news/4447-tinubu_fashola_clash_at_birthday_colloquium.html.

Proctor, Mark. "Faith, Works, and the Christian Religion in James 2:14–26." *Evangelical Quarterly* 69 (1997) 307–22.

Raboteau, Albert J. *Slave Religion: The "Invisible Institution" in the Antebellum South.* New York: Oxford University Press, 1980.

Ray, Benjamin C. *African Traditional Religions: Symbol, Ritual and Community.* Hoboken, NJ: Prentice Hall, 1976.

Richardson, Kurt A. *James.* The New American Commentary 36. Nashville: Broadman & Holman, 1997.

Ropes, J. H. *A Critical and Exegetical Commentary on the Epistle of James. International Critical Commentary.* Edinburgh: T. & T. Clark, 1916.

Schmid, Vernon L. "The Poor: American Outcasts." *Christian Century* 99, 1126–27.

Sidebottom, E. M. *James, Jude, 2 Peter.* New Century Bible Commentary. London: Thomas Nelson, 1967.

Simeon, Charles. *Horae Homileticae: James to Jude, Volume 20.* London: Holdsworth and Ball, 1833.

Skillen, James W. "Covenant, Federalism, and Social Justice." *Annual of the Society of Christian Ethics* 20 (2000) 111–18.

Serrão, C. Jeanne Orjala. *James: A Commentary in the Wesleyan Tradition.* New Beacon Bible Commentary. Kansas City, MO: Beacon Hill, 2010.

Sewakpo, Honore. "The Relevance of James' Attitude Towards Partiality for Nigeria." *African Journal of Biblical Studies* 31 (2013) 97–115.

Sleeper, C. Freeman. *James.* Abingdon New Testament Commentaries. Nashville: Abingdon, 1998.

Smit, D. J. "Exegesis and Proclamation: 'Show No Partiality . . .' (James 2:1–13)." *Journal Of Theology For Southern Africa* 71 (1990) 59–68.

Southey, Robert. *The Life of Wesley: and the Rise and Progress of Methodism.* 1st ed. New York: Routledge, 2022.

Stott, John. *Issues Facing Christians Today.* London: Marshall Pickering, 1984.

Stulac, George M. Source: "Who are 'The Rich' in James?" *Presbyterion* 16 (1990) 89–102.

Tamez, E. "James: A Circular Letter for Immigrants." *Review and Expositor* 108 (2011) 369–80.

———. *The Scandalous Message of James: Faith Without Works Is Dead.* New York: Crossroad, 1990.

Tanner, R. E. S. *Transition in African Belief: A Study in Sukumaland, Tanzania, East Africa.* Maryknoll, NY: Maryknoll, 1967.

Taringa, Nisbert Taisekwa. "African Metaphors for God: Male or Female?" *Scriptura: Journal For Biblical, Theological and Contextual Hermeneutics* 86 (2004) 174–79.

Tarr, Delbart Howard. *Double Image: Biblical Insights from African Parables*. Mahwah, NJ: Paulist, 1994.

Tasker, R. V. G. *The General Epistle of James*. Grand Rapids: Eerdmans, 1974.

Taylor, John V. *Christianity and Politics in Africa*. Harmondsworth: Penguin, 1957.

Tillman, William M., Jr. "Social Justice in the Epistle of James: a New Testament Amos?" *Review and Expositor* 108 (2011) 417–27.

Theissen, Gerd. *Social Reality and the Early Christians: Theology, Ethics, and the World of the New Testament*. Minneapolis: Fortress, 1992.

Thomas, John Christopher. *Devils, Disease, and Deliverance: Origins of Illness in New Testament Thought*. Sheffield: Sheffield Academic, 1998.

Turner, Harold. *Profile through Preaching*. Research Pamphlets 13. London: Edinburgh House, 1965.

Vanhoozer, Kevin J. *Hearers and Doers: A Pastor's Guide to Making Disciples Through Scripture and Doctrine*. Bellingham, WA: Lexham, 2019.

Varner, William. "The Main Theme and the Structure of James." *Master's Seminary Journal* 22 (2011) 115–29.

Vlachos, Chris A. *James (Exegetical Guide to the Greek Text)*. Nashville: Broadman & Holman, 2013.

Walters, J. Michael. *James: A Bible Commentary in the Wesleyan Tradition*. Indianapolis: Wesleyan, 1997.

Warden, Duane. "The Rich and Poor in James: Implications for Institutionalized Partiality." *Journal of the Evangelical Theological Society* 43 (2000) 247–57.

Wesley, John. *Explanatory Notes on the New Testament*. Grand Rapids: Baker, 1983.

Wilson, Walter T. "Sin as Sex and Sex with Sin: The Anthropology of James 1:12–15." *Harvard Theological Review* 95 (2002) 147–68.

Whartenby, Tom. "James 1:17–27." *Interpretation* 63 (2009) 176–78.

Whitlark, Jason A. "*Emphytos Logos*: A New Covenant Motif in the Letter of James." *Horizons In Biblical Theology* 32 (2010) 144–65.

White, James Bliese. "Jubilee: The Basis of Social Action." *Reformed Journal* 21, 8–11.

Williams, Robert Lee. "Piety and Poverty in James." *Wesleyan Theological Journal* 22 (1987) 37–55.

Witherington, Ben, III. *Jesus the Sage: The Pilgrimage of Wisdom*. Minneapolis: Fortress, 1998.

———. *Letters and Homilies for Jewish Christians: A Socio-Rhetorical Commentary on Hebrews, James and Jude*. Downers Grove, IL: InterVarsity, 2007.

Ziegler, John J. "Who Can Anoint the Sick." *Worship* 61 (1987) 25–44.

Ziglar, Toby. "Profit or People First? An Examination of Jas 4:13–16." *Review and Expositor* 108 (2011) 453–58.

———. "When Words Get in the Way of True Religion." *Review and Expositor* 100 (2003) 269–77.